Scalamandré

First Edition
08 07 06 05 04   5 4 3 2 1

Published by
Gibbs Smith, Publisher
P.O. Box 667
Layton, Utah 84041

Orders: 800.748.5439
www.gibbs-smith.com

Designed by Glyph Publishing
Printed and bound in Hong Kong

Photographs:
> Front jacket—"Gustavian Floral" cotton on the ceiling plus thirteen other coordinating
> patterns; interior design by Michael Simon, see p. 28
> Back jacket—Pillow designs by Carol Knott; see p. 122
> Page ii—"Edwin's Covey," a hand-printed union cloth
> Page v—Intricate handmade "Marie Antoinette" silk rosettes in peach, coral and moss hold
> back "Versaille" warp-printed silk curtain panels

Library of Congress Cataloging-in-Publication Data

Coleman, Brian D.
  Scalamandré : luxurious home interiors / Brian D. Coleman ; photography by
Dan Mayers.—1st ed.
     p. cm.
  ISBN 1-58685-408-9
  1. Scalamandré (Firm) 2. Textile fabrics in interior decoration.
  I. Title.
NK2115.5.F3C6497 2004
747'.3—dc22
                              2004008600

Contents

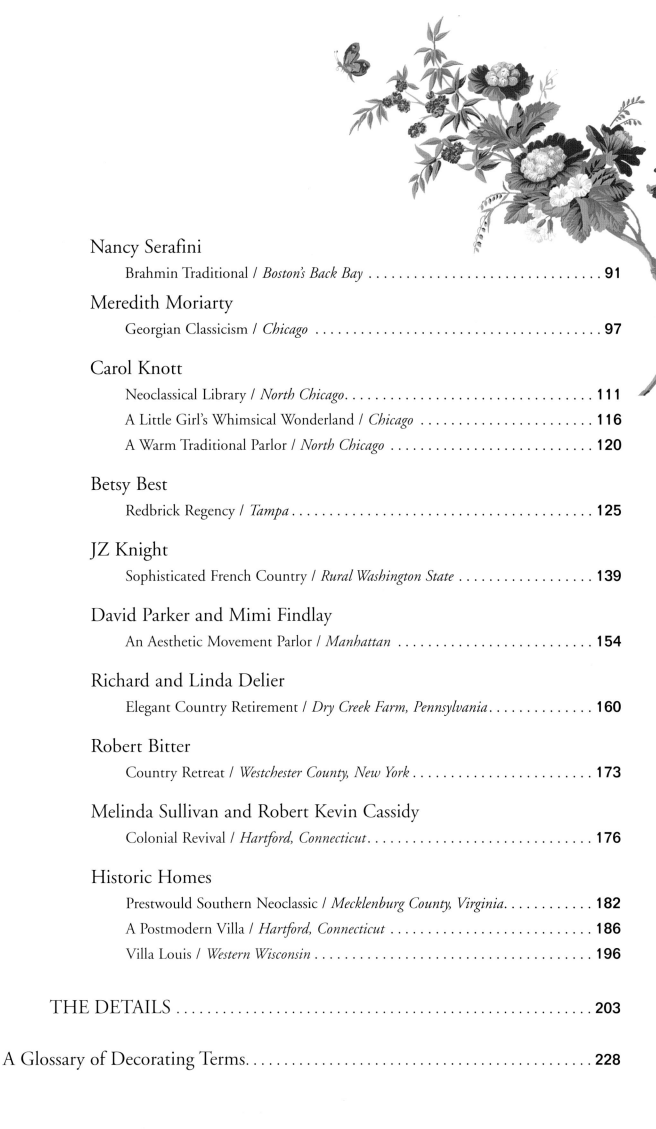

ACKNOWLEDGMENTS

The author and photographer would like to thank the following for their assistance:

This book would not have been possible without the enthusiasm and support of Bob and Mark Bitter, their parents, Adriana and Edwin Bitter, as well as the rest of the Bitter family. Scalamandré's employees were uniformly helpful, in particular Liana Zandomenego and Trish Connolly, who went out of their way to help whenever they could. This book all began with Mark Failor's efforts from the Scalamandré Seattle showroom, and both his and Pat Kreeger's support were much appreciated.

Talented designers and hospitable homeowners around the country are what have made this book so beautiful, and our gratitude to them is heartfelt. Without our agent Julie Castiglia, this book would have never materialized; her constant encouragement and words of wisdom made the whole process easier. Our editor at Gibbs Smith, Publisher, Madge Baird, transformed words and pictures into this beautiful book and was always there when needed. Dan thanks Misha and Lola as well as his parents, Stan and Virginia Mayers, for their support, and Brian thanks Howard for his constant encouragement.

FACING *"Polka Dot," a contemporary acrylic jacquard from the Island Cloth Collection is being woven on a mechanical Jacquard loom.*

Adriana Scalamandré Bitter

Chairman of the Board

The noise of a batten beating in the weft yarn on a shuttle loom is extremely loud, but it was a comforting sound to me. It was the sound of a beautiful product being manufactured, and it seemed to give me a sense of security and a purpose to my life. My memory does not go beyond an intense love of drawing and my father and mother, Franco and Flora Scalamandré, working together to translate old textile documents onto graph paper in preparation to have them woven in our mill in Long Island City, New York. This mill was purchased five years before I was born, and by the time I was ten years old, my father had me hand-painting designs on textiles as my first commission for a client.

Steam rising up from our dye vats, colors being printed one by one on fabrics that we wove, and talented ladies hand-making beautiful tassels were part of my life. I was part of this wonderful place, and my father always gave me a sense of importance. He made my brother and me feel that no decisions would be made in business without our input, and rather than becoming an unwanted burden on our young shoulders, it gave a value to our lives.

Soon after our company was founded by my parents in 1929, a few dedicated women in the world of preservation heard that someone in New York was weaving extraordinary fabrics that would be suitable for the homes they were trying to save. They were Henry

Dupont's sister, Mrs. Crowninshield; Nancy McClelland, a designer and importer of fine wallpapers; and Aunt Annie Smith, of Kenmore. They told my father they would love to be his American aunties if he would only help them in their efforts in the field of preservation. It became a wonderful union that continued for many years.

As my own art skills developed, I was able to help more on the reproduction of textiles, and I not only studied the documents but also analyzed how they were woven, what yarns were used, and which of our looms could reproduce them.

The first Scalamandré showroom I recall was at 598 Madison Avenue, where we expanded to two full floors by the time I reached fifteen years of age. Scalamandré hired traveling salesmen (they were the only men that traveled at that time) to call on clients as the industry expanded throughout the United

States. We were one of the first fabric houses to open a showroom in the Merchandise Mart in Chicago in the '30s, and soon after we opened in California.

My parents traveled to historic homes, and I went along. Eighteenth-century style became more familiar to me than the twentieth-century homes that most people lived in. As we spent so much time in Virginia, where we were the official manufacturers for Historic Williamsburg, I spent many days in the local grammar school, which was quite different from my New York school.

Our company was not *part* of our life, it *was* our life, and our family was the company. Our employees were an extended family, and the documents and designs were my toys.

In all my recollections, there was never a mention of success measured by profit; it was always success based on achieving a goal of correctly reproducing a period textile, of pleasing a client with a beautiful product delivered on time, of creating a new design that was well accepted in the marketplace. Dollars only came into a discussion when there was a need to buy a new loom, to add on a new division—such as wallpaper, and later carpet—or to open a new showroom.

Not long before my father's death in 1988, I asked him why he had given so much to historic homes in America, and he answered me simply and honestly that this new country had given him, an Italian immigrant, an opportunity to build a new life, and it was his way of saying thank you.

The sound of the old shuttle looms will always be in the background for me—not a loud banging, but the music of the continuation of a beautiful silk textile being woven and available to many generations to come.

FACING *Franco Scalamandré and his daughter, Adriana Scalamandré Bitter, translate the artwork for a design to point paper, c. 1960.*

LEFT *Edwin and Adriana Bitter, co-chairs of the board of Scalamandré, and their sons Robert Scalamandré Bitter and Mark Bitter, co-presidents of the company, at the New York showroom, December 2003.*

Robert Bitter

Co-President

For years, our family, friends, and clients have encouraged us to write a Scalamandré book. There always seemed to be so many excuses for not getting it done. We were either too busy, overcommitted, in the middle of a recession or just unable to finance it.

Sometime in 2001, Mark Failor, our Seattle Sales Representative, encouraged me to get together with Brian Coleman, who I was told was a very enthusiastic antique textile collector and the West Coast Editor for *Old House Interiors*. We finally met in New York to share our passion for textiles and to exchange the many stories related to our business. It didn't take long for Brian to say, "Scalamandré has a fascinating history, a beautiful collection, and deserves to have their story told." By then, Brian had earned my confidence, and I responded that if anyone was ever going to make it happen, it was him. Brian's energy and enthusiasm were real and I could sense that his schedules and commitments were sincere.

I was thrilled to realize that we could share our family history and business with a larger audience. Our New York–based family operation was unique, and with the marketplace changing so rapidly, I felt it was critical to capture as much of our legacy as we could. Manufacturing, importing and exporting home furnishings are challenges in their own right, but to color the yarns, wind them, prepare the warps, weave, finish, hand print the papers and fabrics, and

Flora and Franco Scalamandré, c. 1962, hold "Madison," a red-and-gold silk lampas sofa medallion woven for Jacqueline Kennedy and used in the Red Room of the White House.

produce the trimmings to match—all under one roof in North America—makes Scalamandré one of a kind. In addition to having a vertical manufacturing operation, it was decided years ago that we would control our own distribution channels and sell through our own wholesale showrooms. I have always been fascinated by the complexity of our operation and am, quite frankly, amazed that for seventy-five years the business has carried on.

As children, it was not uncommon for us to be picked up by "Nonno" and "Nonna" on the weekend, stopping off at the Manhasset Diner, and then ending up at the Long Island City mill. Paperwork and point papers were never ending, and our grandparents and parents loved to teach us about their work. We always enjoyed visiting the mill. The best part for us was exploring the many workshops and trying to figure out how all the crazy devices worked.

It was perfectly normal for us to hear about business around the dinner table. Special orders, prestigious clients and unexpected challenges were discussed regularly, both at home and with our grandparents. It wasn't unusual for our family to visit clients, antiques shops or historic homes during our vacations or travels. My siblings and I learned to appreciate these experiences and grew to understand that the interesting people and places we would encounter were the "perks" of our family business.

During high school and college, I was lucky enough to be asked to help out with the various work projects in our Long Island City mill. I often wondered if we were truly helping out or whether our parents just wanted to keep an eye on us. I always enjoyed meeting and working with the colorful personalities in our mill, many of whom I had known my entire life. I have always liked being on a first-name basis with our employees.

Soon after my graduation from Boston College, I was officially asked to join the company and report to the mill. I had visions of a grand office and sweeping views, so when I walked into my grandparents' office and saw my grandfather, my father and my brother Ward crowded into one office, I knew I needed a reality check. It came very fast as my father offered me a spot on a hat rack and told me that I might be lucky to get an office in a few years. Oh, well. The welcoming party was not as I had anticipated, but I was happy to be involved and was ready to roll up my sleeves.

The dynamics within a family business are most likely different for every individual involved; however, it is safe to say that an extra layer of complexity is added to the work experience. I consider myself extremely lucky to have grown up in the world of textiles and to have worked in such a respected company. Of course, there have been short periods of trauma, but most of my career has been tremendously rewarding.

The personnel of the Scalamandré mill are pictured in front of the trim floor yarns in November 2003. Many of the nearly one hundred employees are second- and third-generation employees of Scalamandré. OVERLEAF *Hand-woven bullion fringe is still produced on a late-nineteenth-century hand loom.*

The challenges of running a multifaceted textile company are endless—each day bombarded with questions and deadlines—but, thankfully, the pleasure of getting together in the mill as artisans and working together to help solve the needs of the design trade is highly rewarding. The satisfaction of conceptualizing with talented designers and being able to bring those ideas to life in design, color, texture and weaves is what motivates us to push on. Yes, there are factors such as payrolls, mortgages and the bottom line to be managed, but it is the tradition of quality work within the decorative arts field that inspires the employees at Scalamandré.

Our family business is extremely proud of both Brian Coleman and Dan Mayers for completing the first book on Scalamandré. Brian's orchestration and design sensitivity combined with Dan's photographic talents create an entertaining view of our company and the luxurious home environments that are the end result of our efforts. Readers get to see not only the historic looms that produce our elegant fabrics and trims but also many of the private interiors enhanced by our textiles. On behalf of all the Scalamandré and Bitter families, *"grazie mille."*

The Scalamandré Story

In the world of textiles, the name Scalamandré stands out as one of the premier manufacturers of fine fabrics and trimmings in the United States. Since 1929, Scalamandré has been weaving its own exquisite silks, wools, linens and cottons, as well as laboriously hand making elaborate and ornate trims, cordings, tiebacks and fringes (called *passementerie,* the French term for the decorative trimmings) for some of the finest interiors in the country. Discovered by early preservationists in the 1930s, Scalamandré has also had the unique role of being the

major manufacturer of historical fabrics in the United States and over the years has woven historically accurate textiles for restorations ranging from the Red Room of the White House to William Morris's home, Kelmscott, in England.

Founded by Franco Scalamandré, the company is also unique in that it has remained a family business since the beginning, and today the third generation of the family continues to run the company, which is still based in a historic brick mill outside of Manhattan.

From the beginning, Scalamandré's attention to superb color and fine detail is what has set it apart from other textile manufacturers. And even though Scalamandré uses period looms and hand work, this is now combined with state-of-the-art computers and high-speed electronic Jacquard looms to replicate and enhance the wonderful textiles of the past.

In the twenty-first century, Scalamandré remains at the forefront of textile design and manufacture. A new flagship showroom in Manhattan was opened in the fall of 2003 in the D & D Annex to showcase the Scalamandré collection of soft furnishings. Scalamandré continues to manufacture many of its products itself, which makes it unique among textile manufacturers in the United States. Recently the company has begun expansion of its American-made products by opening another mill in South Carolina, with the goal of keeping the textile industry alive in this country.

The Scalamandré story began in 1923, when Europe was in the throes of political unrest. Nowhere was this more so than in Italy, as rallies supporting Mussolini were being held in town squares across the country. Many young Italians were disillusioned with Il Duce, and one of those young men was Franco Scalamandré. Aged twenty-six, Franco had been well educated, raised in a military family in southern Italy in the town of Caserta, the center of the Italian silk industry. Franco had served on the front lines during World War I, after which he graduated from college in Naples with a degree in engineering and worked for two years in Egypt. Following a face-to-face confrontation with Mussolini, however, he realized he would either need to emigrate or face certain imprisonment.

Seeing no choice, Franco joined five other fellow engineers and set sail from southern Italy early in 1923 with just his fencing foil and his best opera suit in his bag—the bare necessities, he thought, for making a new life for himself in the land of opportunity.

Life in America was more difficult, however, than Franco had imagined. Italian newspapers had been full of ads for jobs in the United States, but these turned out to be menial labor positions in large factories—not at all what he had envisioned for himself. And although he had been trained as an engineer, Franco's poor English made it hard for him at first to find work in his field. After a series of labor jobs, he did finally find positions as an engineer at Westinghouse and several other manufacturers.

The director of the New York Metropolitan Opera befriended Franco in those early years, and he was able to use his formal opera suit after all, attending some of his favorite Italian operas in New York.

Once he improved his command of the English language, Franco found more challenging positions, first as a draftsman and then as a teacher of architectural design at the Sealey School of Interior Design in New York. Always an entrepreneur, Franco decided to form a new company with Mrs. Sealey's assistance, importing fine furnishings and fabrics directly from Italy. Realizing that there were a limited number of high-end silk manufacturers in the United States, Franco knew he could have a corner on the American silk market if he opened his own mill. With just one weaver and a single loom, Franco began operations in Patterson, New Jersey, in 1927, producing his own silk fabric.

The years before the Great Depression were prosperous ones; demand for fine-quality goods was high and Franco's business took off quickly. By 1929, he was able to save

ABOVE *An employee works on a ruffing machine, which makes the ruffs for ball fringes and bullions, c. 1945.*

FACING, ABOVE *"Scalamandré Silks" stills shines on the side of the company's redbrick mill in Long Island City.*

FACING, BELOW *Franco examines a Jacquard loom at the mill, c. 1960.*

$5,000—enough money for the down payment on an old, half-block-long, redbrick textile mill in Long Island City, just across the river from bustling Manhattan. Franco called his new company Scalamandré Silks, after his family name. And thus began what would become one of the foremost manufacturers of fine textiles and trimmings in the United States.

Franco met Daisy Baranzelli on one of his Atlantic crossings to import Italian goods, and she invited him home to meet her sister Flora. A descendant of an old Italian family of artists, Flora was the daughter of a successful sculptor, and Franco was enchanted with her beauty and artistic skills. The two were married in 1929, and Franco and Flora found they were not only a good matrimonial match but also very well suited to the entrepreneurial endeavor of running the textile company. Flora used her experience as an artist to become an expert colorist and designer of fabrics, while Franco's training in engineering was invaluable as he took on the task of running the mill. Franco studied antique textiles and adapted old looms to reproduce them. They began hiring Italian and other European weavers who were trained to work on Jacquard looms, and bought machinery for winding, quilling and warping, as well as cutting jacquard cards, so that all phases of design and weaving could be done at the mill. A trimmings manufacturer already in the mill was absorbed into the new company, and a dye house was added within several years. It wasn't long before the company had expanded to occupy the entire 50,000 square feet of the building.

A delicate silk liseré covered with a pattern of whimsical strawberries was one of their first productions and an immediate success, bought by designers throughout the country for

fine interiors, including the White House. Franco had always had a good sense of style, and to celebrate their first wedding anniversary as well as the success of their new company, he presented his bride and business partner with a sparkling ruby pin fashioned into a strawberry, a token of their very first and quite successful creation.

Nineteen twenty-nine was generally not a good year to begin a new business, as the Roaring Twenties came to a screeching halt that October with the crash of the stock market. While many companies soon succumbed to the uncertain economy, Franco continued right on, never afraid to look adversity directly in the eye. The depression, he was fond of saying, was actually a wonderful time to start his business, as materials and labor were so inexpensive. And Franco was not afraid to roll up his sleeves and pitch right in. Adriana Scalamandré Bitter, Franco's daughter and today co-chair of the board of Scalamandré, likes to recall her father's stories of how, during the depression, he would load rolls of silk into the back of his station wagon, then drive from one end of the eastern seaboard to the other, making sales calls from Maine to Atlanta, often sleeping on the fabrics in the back of the car. Franco's efforts paid off, as his company's reputation as one of the premier sources for fine textiles in the country spread.

By the early 1930s, as more and more designers and architects became familiar with the quality and beauty of Scalamandré's silks, Franco was approached to reproduce historic textiles. In 1932, French and Company, the decorating firm involved in the major renovation of San Simeon for

ABOVE *Franco Scalamandré with his grandsons (from left) Robert Bitter and Ward Bitter and their cousin Franco Scalamandré examine a strike-off from a flatbed screen of neoclassical wallpaper, c. 1965.* FACING, ABOVE *A 5/8 inch silk gimp in the process of being woven. Notice the quill being carried by the shuttle.* FACING, BELOW *Flora Scalamandré working on the design of a damask, c. 1958.*

William Randolph Hearst and his actress girlfriend Marion Davies asked Franco to weave just seven yards of an antique brocatelle for a project. The brocatelle, the designers told Franco, was a rare fifteenth-century material and the reproduction would have to match the original perfectly. Franco examined the textile and then informed the decorators that he would be happy to replicate it, adding that although they had been sold the fabric as antique, it was in reality no more than fifty years old. And so Franco designed and wove the brocatelle (at a cost of $1,000 per yard), even making special looms for the project. Franco washed the finished fabric to help give it some age and hung it overnight on the roof of his building to dry. But a freak March storm that night buried the roof in snow. Fortunately, when Franco dug out his precious fabric the next morning, he was amazed to find that instead of ruining the brocatelle, the snow had aged it perfectly, and it was now an exact

match for the original! French and Company, as well as Mr. Hearst and Ms. Davies, were delighted. Franco's career in restoration of historic textiles had begun.

Word of Franco's skills in restoration soon spread, and Louise du Pont Crowninshield, a pioneer American preservationist and the sister of Henry du Pont, approached Franco to help reproduce documentary fabrics for historic houses. Franco was delighted to help and spared no expense or detail: for example, he built a special handloom to exactly replicate an eighteenth-century French lampas for Colonial Williamsburg.

At Mount Vernon, frustrated preservationists could not find any traces of the historic fabrics until Franco suggested they look in mouse holes, as mice often steal bits of fabric for their nests. A small scrap of dimity was found behind a bedroom wall in this manner, after which Franco reproduced it for its original use as a bed hanging. (The dimity remains in the Scalamandré collection today.)

Scalamandré established itself as a leader in the restoration of historic textiles in the United States, having contributed over the years to hundreds of projects ranging from Philadelphia's Congress Hall to the White House. Franco often said that helping in restorations was his way of paying back his adopted country for his precious gift of freedom.

During World War II, many American textile mills were forced to close due to a shortage of raw materials. Not so for Scalamandré. During a trip to Italy in 1939, Franco realized that war was imminent and wisely foresaw that it would soon be impossible to purchase raw silk. He quickly returned to the States and, fortunately, was able to purchase and stockpile silk made in China, thereby ensuring that his company would stay in business during the war. Scalamandré was even able to sell some of its stockpile surplus to other American manufacturers. The company converted 80 percent of its operations to wartime goods, making sergeants' silk stripes, campaign ribbons (the military ordered rayon but Franco insisted on giving them

ABOVE *Edwin Ward Bitter, Robert Franco Scalamandré Bitter, and Tami Bitter Cook pose with a reproduction of William Morris's "Bird" wool ingrain as it is woven on a Scotch ingrain loom.*

LEFT *Ameer Khan laboriously hand wraps silk cord in "Cord Alley."*

silk), silk parachute ribbons (noted for their strength), linings for combat helmets, braid for WACs' caps, and even camouflage nets.

Following World War II, Scalamandré discontinued its production of war products but continued making designer textiles and increased its trimmings as well, which were becoming more and more popular. In the 1950s, it added wallpaper lines. The first design center in the country, Chicago's Merchandise Mart, had opened in 1930, and Scalamandré opened its first fabric showroom soon afterwards. As design centers grew in popularity in the 1950s and 1960s, Scalamandré expanded to additional cities, gaining recognition as one of the country's leading manufacturers of fine fabrics and trimmings.

The simplest way to understand how the Jacquard machine works is to think of the operation of a player piano. In the player piano, a paper roll with holes punched in it moves across a special cylinder. As the holes cross the cylinder, they cause various keys to depress and strike the notes.

Similarly, in a Jacquard machine, a chain of up to 12,000 cards, each one specially punched according to a pattern, moves around a cylinder. As they cross the cylinder, little fingers pop through wherever there is a hole. These fingers then cause long wires, each with a hook on its end, to lift. As they do so, the wires catch various warp threads, lifting them to form a shed; and then the shuttle shoots through between the raised threads and those that lie below, carrying a filler yarn to pass through. This intersection of yarn at right angles creates the fabric.

Alonzo repairs a broken silk warp thread on the backside of the Jacquard loom.

Franco and Flora Scalamandré's two children, Gino and Adriana, began working in the company while they were young. Adriana, an artist like her mother, did many of the historic reproductions and became one of the company's most proficient artists, being able to translate a document to graph paper and then hand-cut jacquard cards for the Jacquard looms, a very detailed process taking months of painstaking, exacting work.

In 1954, Adriana married Edwin Bitter, who decided to leave the navy to join the family business. Adriana and Edwin raised four children and in 1969 purchased the remaining shares of Scalamandré stock from other family members, dedicating themselves to the business. Adriana focused her talents in product design, while Edwin was in charge of sales. Their children were also involved from an early age in planning and business decisions, and by the 1980s all four had joined the firm: Ward focused on sales and marketing, Bob in production

development, Mark in production, and Tami as an architect who handled facility planning and design.

Although Flora Scalamandré died in 1987 and Franco a few months later in 1988, the clattering looms, steaming dye vats, and hand-woven trimmings all remain. Scalamandré continues in the forefront of design, adding new lines, such as its Island Cloth Collection of acrylic outdoor fabrics. The popular traditional designs remain in production as well, from classic Italian silk damasks to handmade passementerie. The latest in computer-aided production is now used alongside the turn-of-the-twentieth-century looms and the skilled hand craftsmanship of its artisans. Franco and Flora Scalamandré would be proud to see their grandchildren today as they carry on the family's tradition, ensuring that Scalamandré continues to produce the finest in textiles and trimmings for a discerning clientele.

LEFT *Jesus Jimenez is hand printing "Lady Skipworth's Garden," a late-eighteenth-century hand-blocked wallpaper reproduced by Scalamandré for Prestwould Plantation in Clarksville, Virginia.*

BELOW *Fringe is slowly and carefully made by hand, as Luz Maria Lopez attaches silk-wrapped molds to a silk heading.*

FACING *Silk in every color of the rainbow is available stored on wooden spools.*

ABOVE   *A collection of skeins and spools of chenille in a wide range of colors, from golds to reds to blues, awaits use on a table in the mill.*

FACING   *Even the empty wooden warp spools used to store the delicate silk have a beauty of their own.*

Scalamandré Homes

We have chosen a selection of homes from around the country to show how Scalamandré fabrics, trimmings and wallpapers are being used today. Interiors range from a simple, colorful cottage in Colorado to a grand and formal, French-inspired interior on Fifth Avenue in New York. Each is unique, reflecting the interests and lifestyle of its owners; but what all have in common is a strong sense of style, a love of color, and an enthusiasm for good design.

Interior designers have been the guiding force for each of these homes, and so we begin by visiting with the designers, followed by a visual journey into the beauty of Scalamandré, from pillows and portieres to poolside chaises.

A vintage apron rests on the breakfast room chair, which was hand-painted with a rabbit motif. The chair seat is covered with Scalamandré "Jubilee" striped jacquard in celery, wine and ecru, with green-and-pink cording and tassel trim in off-white, burgundy, shell and grass green. Interior design by JZ Knight.

MICHAEL SIMON

Michael Simon is one of New York's most highly sought-after designers. Known for his love of formal French elegance, Simon has designed some of the top interiors around the country. Initially a composer, Simon decided to follow his other passion in life—interior design—and the early 1990s began what has become a very successful second career. Simon has worked with Scalamandré on many projects. He designed their New York showroom in 1994, including a striking window display of eighteenth-century French antiques upholstered with fabrics and trims that were woven to look as if they had oxidized over the centuries. This project helped establish Simon in the design community, and he has since received important commissions from around the country. We look at three of his favorite interiors, beginning with one of his earliest—a fashionable apartment in Philadelphia.

Louis XV Elegance

PHILADELPHIA

Michael Simon designed this fashionable apartment on Rittenhouse Square in Philadelphia in 1991. The entire apartment was gutted and the owners moved into a hotel for eight months during the project. The procession through the apartment, from the entrance hall to the living room at the rear, was designed in a palette that could be varied from light to dark to help maintain visual interest. Rich colors of shrimp, coral, oyster, apple green and slate blue were chosen, all of which appear in Scalamandré's colorful silk print "Pomegranate." This fabric was used for the curtains in the living room as well as a skirt for a center table, while Scalamandré's silk taffeta and repp "Shirred Stripe" in pale coral and oyster provided a complementary accent for balloon shades underneath the draperies.

Furniture was French, of course, including a pair of Louis XV fauteuils that were covered in a pale shrimp Scalamandré damask. A tearoom was created at one end of the long room, incorporating

In an apartment' overlooking downtown Philadelphia. Scalamandré's "Pomegranate" printed silk was used for the draperies, then repeated on the center table's skirt to help bring the eye forward. A collection of Louis XV and XVI furnishings rests on an Aubusson carpet whose colors complement the Scalamandré fabric.

eighteenth-century painted French panels in a boiserie. A restful spot for an early morning cup of coffee or an afternoon tea, the space is centered on a Louis XV card table and chairs that are covered in a custom Scalamandré gauffraged velvet and a Louis XVI canapé covered in Scalamandré's woven lampas "Imperatrice."

The dining room, one of the first rooms opening off the long entrance hall, shimmers in the rosy glow of walls covered with a chinoiserie toile, "Nippon," which was custom printed by Scalamandré in a sanguine colorway on a buff ground. Two different Scalamandré taffetas in coral and ivory were sewn together in wide stripes for the curtains. And what makes the room special is the opulent, parcel-gilded pelmet over the window that was constructed with a taffeta valance accented by individual Chinese characters cut out and appliquéd onto the fabric. Louis XV dining chairs have been covered in a custom Scalamandré coral velvet that was then gauffraged. The dining table is laid with a simple, shrimp-colored woven table cover.

Several bedrooms, a library, and a striking powder room centered on a pair of tabourets covered in Scalamandré "Leopardo" silk-faced velvet complete the apartment. ❧

LEFT *Eighteenth-century French painted paneling was used to create this tearoom alcove at one end of the drawing room. A canapé covered in "Imperatrice" and two side chairs covered in custom, gauffraged coral velvet flank a Louis XV table, set for tea. A rock crystal-and-Meissen porcelain chandelier hangs overhead.*

ABOVE *Scalamandré's silk taffeta and repp "Shirred Stripe," used for the balloon shades, is repeated on this sofa pillow.*

LEFT   The alternating stripes of taffeta are complemented by undercurtains of Scalamandré striped silk taffeta in a custom coral colorway. A Scalamandré tasseled fringe highlights the overcurtains.

ABOVE   The dining room glows with the rosy coral color of Scalamandré's chinoiserie toile "Nippon." Fanciful Oriental figures were cut out of the toile and appliquéd onto the valance that tops the opulent curtains. Constructed of alternating wide strips of Scalamandré taffetas in coral and ivory, the curtains give the room a warm, sensual look. A Louis XV crystal chandelier hangs overhead. The dining chairs are also Louis XV, covered with a custom Scalamandré gauffraged velvet.

FACING   The powder room off the drawing room is papered in a baroque-patterned wallpaper. A pair of tabourets is covered in Scalamandré "Leopardo" silk-faced velvet. A nineteenth-century Venetian mirror and American crystal wall sconces hang above a Louis XV–style console that has been fashioned into a vanity.

DECORATING

Finders Keepers

Designer Ashley Hanley brings all her favorite things into one place–the 1939 Richmond, Virginia, charmer she calls home

BY JOANNA LINBERG

ALL THE RIGHT LINES
In her daughter Louise's room, which is the smallest in the house, Hanley thought ahead to when it might one day be a guest space, choosing the versatile Cambridge Stripe wallpaper from Cole & Son.

photographs by JAMES RANSOM

ASHLEY HANLEY is probably in an antiques store right now. The Virginia interior designer (shown above) knows that you can't fake a layered, curated look, so she puts in the time—searching the shelves in out-of-the-way thrift shops, making friends with dealers at consignment stores, and tracking auction listings online to get pieces that give each of her clients' homes a style that can't be replicated.

About three years ago, her constant hunt paid off. While on a run in a neighborhood near downtown Richmond, Hanley spotted a 1939 brick house with an estate-sale sign out front. For once, she skipped the bargains and called her Realtor instead to see if the place would be on the market soon.

"This was during COVID times, when we were living in a small 1940s home. We'd recently had our second child and were feeling very cramped," she says. The four-bedroom house with an addition on the back meant extra breathing space for her and her husband, Brendan, as well as their growing family. After they wrote a personal letter explaining their wish to honor the architectural style—a pleasing mix of Georgian, Colonial, and Federal—it was miraculously theirs for under the asking price. Hanley had scored her best find yet.

"It was just meant to be," she says. "We wanted an older house with lots of character, one that would also be a little bit of a fixer-upper so we could put our own spin on it." True to her letter, Hanley left the structure almost exactly as she found it and focused her renovation energy on true trouble spots, updating a timeworn main-hall bath and transforming the third floor from a mirror-lined man cave into a whimsical playroom for her two young daughters, Frances Miller and Louise.

Trading Spaces

"We swapped the living and dining rooms because we love to entertain and our families are here in town," says Hanley. "Switching those gave us space to host them." The table is from a local shop, but the real coup is the crystal chandelier. The designer saw it online and bid on it, not expecting to win. She did, so she went to Philadelphia to get it. "Talk about a nerve-racking drive home!" she recalls.

The Elegance of Versailles

FIFTH AVENUE, NEW YORK

The owners of this spectacular apartment on New York's Fifth Avenue were just looking for a simple pied-à-terre in the city, but when they discovered this magnificent space, they couldn't resist it. Soaring eighteen-foot ceilings covered with ornate plasterwork dotted with putti and arabesques accent the ornately carved wall paneling and a richly sculpted marble fireplace. The room seems like an opera set—perfect for the owner, who is a former opera singer. The building, overlooking Central Park, was commissioned by Julius Berwind at the turn of the twentieth century as a single family residence. The interiors were designed by the noted Philadelphia architect Horace Trumbauer. Known for his opulent interiors (for example, the Berwinds' famous mansion in Newport, The Elms), Trumbauer spared no expense for this Fifth Avenue home, incorporating ornate paneling and plasterwork in all of the public rooms.

By the time the current owners found their apartment in 1998, each floor had been divided into separate apartments—theirs serving as the home's reception rooms, including the ballroom and smoking room on the second floor. Previous owners had painted the walls a dingy green and filled the rooms with art deco furniture. Simon began the apartment's restoration by brightening its palette with a period-appropriate cream, rose, celadon green and gold color scheme. Scalamandré was called upon to provide samples from their archives of fabrics that had been woven at the turn of the twentieth century and might have been found in this type of grand interior. One of these textiles, "The Elms," immediately caught Simon's attention, as its scale and pattern looked perfect for the room. This fabric was, in fact,

Fit for a stage, the grand salon is highlighted by ornate plaster carvings of cavorting putti. Simon had the room painted in serene tones of cream and gold, and added draperies in a Scalamandré rose silk taffeta. Austrian shades in the cream silk taffeta "Elegante" add privacy. Walls are covered in Scalamandré "The Elms" silk-and-cotton damask, and the sofas are covered in the same material. A celadon "Brocart de Lyon" brocade from Scalamandré was used to upholster a pair of Louis XV bergeres at the end of the room.

commissioned by Julius Berwind for his Newport residence, The Elms, and might even have been used in his Fifth Avenue mansion.

The redecoration started with the rug, and after much searching, a nineteenth-century Austrian Savonnerie in shades of pink was found to provide a perfect contrast to the heavily plastered ceiling. Rose, celadon, ivory and a series of pinks were chosen as the color scheme and textiles were selected. Curtains in a Scalamandré rose taffeta were installed, with Austrian shades in "Elegante," an ivory silk taffeta. The silk damask "The Elms" was custom woven in cream and used to upholster the walls, and the sofas were also covered in the same material. Two pairs of large bergeres were upholstered in Scalamandré's celadon "Brocart de Lyon" brocade.

The former smoking room was made into the bedroom, centered on an extravagant canopied bed designed by Simon. Based on beds from the eighteenth century in the Louis XVI taste, the bed took ten tradesmen more than a year to construct. Scalamandré referenced an eighteenth-century brocade that was made into a cotton print entitled "French Garlands" for upholstered walls, windows and bed hangings.

LEFT *Cushions in warp-printed taffeta in rose and ivory rest on the sofa. A custom-figured galloon offsets the curtains.*

ABOVE *Ornate plasterwork and wood detailing give the room a grand and opulent look. The curtains are in a Scalamandré silk rose taffeta.*

FACING *A bergere covered in Scalamandré's celadon "Brocart de Lyon" brocade rests at one end of the salon.*

LEFT *Swags and garlands of roses were taken from the Scalamandré cotton print and hand appliquéd onto the headboard and bed cover, which were then quilted and trapuntoed. Custom apricot silk curtains from Scalamandré were used as undercurtains for both the bed and the windows.*

FACING *The bedroom is centered on a canopied bed designed by Simon and fits the grand space perfectly. The walls, windows and bed curtains are covered with the custom cotton print "French Garlands" by Scalamandré, adapted from an eighteenth-century documentary French textile.*

FACING *Smocking gathers the "Shirred Stripe" taffeta in celadon at the dressing table, which looks out onto Fifth Avenue and Central Park.*

ABOVE *A detail of the headboard shows the appliquéd floral design, highlighted against the vermicular-quilted silk faille—all done by hand.*

Sweet and Light Gustavian Aerie

THE MIDWEST

One of Michael Simon's most complicated undertakings, this new master suite addition to a substantial home in the Midwest was conceived as a private suite for the owners, whose love of the simple and bright look of Swedish design was the project's starting point.

A Gustavian aerie was conceived, with a mansard roof punctuated by oeil-de-boeuf windows, French doors and a simple painted floor. Drawings of Swedish and French flowers from the eighteenth century were researched and patterns devised, even incorporating a Chinese artist engaged in drawing the flowers and vines; more than fourteen custom designs in total were created for the room.

The palette was one of soft pinks, yellows and greens cast in a dusty tonality for a sophisticated sensibility. The latest technology was utilized: the fabric on the walls was inkjet printed in Italy under Scalamandré's supervision. An eighteenth-century French mantel was found and its carved frieze of entwining vines used as a motif throughout the room, from curtain borders, bed-linen embroidery, and floor painting to water jet–cut marble borders and etched glass in the master bath.

Repetition of patterns, in fact, is one of Simon's favorite design tools, and a vermicelli-like patterned cotton, "Blair Sprig," was used as a "rails and stiles" border on the upholstered walls of the room. "Blair Sprig" is repeated again as a woven silk damask in the dressing room curtains. The headboard and Gustavian chairs are covered in Scalamandré's key lime "Shirred Stripe." The sofa in front of the windows is covered in a dusty pink custom damask, "Stratford." ❧

Filled with light, the master suite's spaciousness is emphasized with the angle of the mansard roof. An eighteenth-century Swedish crystal-and-gilt-bronze chandelier hangs in the center. Scalamandré designed the cotton "Gustavian Floral" for the ceiling, plus thirteen coordinating patterns, and had it inkjet printed in Italy to Simon's specifications. Large windows overlook trees and a lake in the distance.

FACING   *The eighteenth-century French-style bed is set with linens embroidered with the floral vine motif; Scalamandré's celadon "Shirred Stripe" was used for the head and footboard coverings. A Gustavian bench rests at the foot of the bed. Scalamandré's ivory taffeta was used for the bed's overcurtains.*

LEFT   *A finely carved eighteenth-century French mantel is the focal point of the front of the room. The carvings of entwining vines were used as a motif for details throughout.*

BELOW   *Detail of the bed canopy shows the delicately carved floral swags that crown its top. "Gustavian Floral," designed from eighteenth-century Swedish and French motifs, was inkjet printed on cotton for upholstering the ceiling. The trim on the bed hangings is accented by the entwining vines of the printed galloon "Laurel, Vine and Bows," its motif derived from the carving in the frieze of the mantel.*

ABOVE *A small guest bath nearby is also covered in Scalamandré's beige wallpaper "Shibui," complemented by "Shimmer Silk" striped taffeta curtains.*

LEFT *Simon commissioned a hand-painted pillow as a gift for the owners. It rests on a sofa that is covered in "Stratford," a dusty pink damask from Scalamandré. Sofa cushions are trimmed in a companion cut-silk fringe.*

FACING *The light-filled master bath adjoining the bedroom looks over a lake and trees. A marble statue of a Grecian maiden is the focal point of the room. Curtains are in a Scalamandré dusty pink taffeta.*

LEFT   *The private sitting room is covered in a deep blue figured velvet.*

ABOVE   *A detail of curtains constructed in "Toledo," a custom silk-and-cotton lampas in a rich copper and blues colorway. The "Toledo" design was inspired by the dress worn by Eleanora di Toledo in her portrait by the late Italian Renaissance painter Bronzino.*

JOAN KRUSE ROGERS

Joan is a product of the Midwest, she likes to explain, with its simple, open spaces that taught her early on that life was an open-ended opportunity. Her first toys were art supplies, and Joan continued her interest in art and design in school, obtaining a bachelor's degree in textiles and interior design at Colorado Women's College. She then pursued advanced studies in architecture, textiles and paint finishes in both the United States and London. Joan has built successful design businesses wherever she has lived, from London to San Antonio to Seattle, which is now her home. Her trademark is her skill at mixing old and new—contemporary and antique—furnishings in her designs, and combining them with skillfully blended colors. Joan enjoys helping homeowners who share a passion for their surroundings in their search for unique and custom designs.

Country French Serenity in a Norman Revival

SEATTLE

Joan likes to design homes that reflect her clients' interests. In this 1930s Norman Revival home overlooking Lake Washington in Seattle, the clients were a young family with three active children, who wanted a sophisticated but tailored home that would be comfortable for their family and also for entertaining. A substantial addition was designed to enlarge the house and open the rooms to the views of Lake Washington and the Cascade Mountains. The master bedroom was part of the new addition, and care was taken to ensure that it blended seamlessly with the

The master bedroom is part of a new addition to the Norman Revival home and now one of the family's favorite spots. "Pillement Toile" wallpaper in a sage colorway coordinates perfectly with the French provincial furnishings. A custom headboard was upholstered in "Pillement Toile" linen, as well, with shirred borders and a flat field. A duvet for the bed and throw cushions in "Pillement Toile" matches the rest of the room. The carpet was kept simple, made in a custom wool blend to harmonize with the French-walnut-stained floors. Curtain treatments were constructed of Scalamandré's printed linen "Pillement Toile," with attractive valances. Other English and French fabrics were selected to coordinate, including pillows, bed valance, Marcella and French settee upholstery.

LEFT   *Cushions in "Pillement Toile" were made to complement the soft green plaid of the settee and creamy whites of the Marcella and bed linens.*

FACING   *Scalamandré's "Pillement Toile" in sage wallpaper lines the hall leading to the master bedroom and sets the stage for the bedroom beyond. Simple and light furnishings, including white wooden shutters and a plain wool sisal rug, emphasize the airy look.*

original home by including features such as arched doorways, a French limestone fireplace, antique silver wall sconces, hardwood floors, and antique cremone pewter bolt hardware. Ten-foot-high ceilings accommodate dramatic drapery treatments, a priority of the clients.

The original architect's blueprints called for large expanses of French doors and windows but left little room for their dressings, so, wisely, several windows were eliminated. Space was made for elegant curtains in Scalamandré's linen print "Pillement Toile"—adapted from an eighteenth-century French design—in a cool and soothing sage green, perfect for the light-filled room. Matching valances were lined with "Festival III," a Scalamandré linen that is weighted just right for both curtain lining and sheers, which were added to protect the room from direct sunlight and the reflection from the lake without disrupting the view.

"Pillement Toile" wallpaper as used and the same pattern was selected in cotton for the custom-made headboard, which was accented with a shirred border and flat field for contrast. A duvet and pillows were also designed in the matching toile. Several English and French cottons and linens in tones of creams and greens were selected for pillows and furniture to complement the toile. A Dublin chair by Scalamandré, upholstered in their ottoman fabric "Stoddard," was selected as a comfortable addition to the room.

Hardwood floors were colored in French walnut and then covered with a simple wool sisal carpet to continue the light and airy feeling. French-walnut furniture, including a commode and armoire, helps tie the room together.

Overall, the bedroom is now one of the family's favorite spaces, and the wife can often be found at the writing desk by the window, enjoying the view of the lake, and sometimes the whole family curls up on the settee and bed to watch a movie. Serene, comfortable, and filled with light, this master bedroom with a Country French elegance reflects the sophistication of a young family and is enjoyed by them all.

CASS DALEY

Cass Daley is a talented designer who began life in another field—sewing and the world of high-fashion design. Her mother first interested her in sewing when she was just nine years old, teaching Cass how to sew on her Girl Scout badge, and by the age of ten she had already won a national competition. Cass soon began sewing for herself and others, becoming an expert in the needle arts, from embroidery to needlepoint, and continuing her interests through her education to the obtaining of a master's in fashion design. Cass has worked in haute couture for twenty-five years, designing and sewing for organizations ranging from the Miss America Beauty Pageant to Christian Dior, and also has sewn clothing for television personalities and international royalty, all of whom appreciate her hand detailing and sense of color and design. Cass has also found a niche as a world-class events organizer, producing more than 500 weddings around the world, from Hong Kong to the Hamptons.

Soon Cass began helping with her wedding clients' home décor. With studios in New York and Colorado, she consults on interiors from Paris to Manhattan. Cass's trademark is producing designs that reflect the personalities and taste of her clients, emphasizing an extraordinary attention to handiwork and detail resulting in rooms with the look of expertly crafted haute couture. Cass's needlework skills often come into play, and she has no hesitation embroidering a pillow or needle pointing a chair cover to add that extra touch; her hand-sewn window treatments are some of the most intricate and finely crafted to be found.

Much of what Cass does is not glamorous, she reminds, just hard work, whether it's designing and sewing a custom gown or a window treatment. Her design philosophy, however, is simple: Cass does what she loves to do, tries to do it better than anyone else, and never stops until everything has been finished to perfection.

We visit one of Cass's favorite projects, the home of collectors of Aesthetic movement antiques in New York, where Cass has been able to blend her needlework skills and expert sense of color and design to create unique custom interiors. And then we will visit her own cottage in Colorado, where she has added cheerful, colorful Scalamandré fabrics to create a delightfully simple rustic setting.

The library is furnished with a collection of nineteenth-century Hunzinger chairs that Cass reupholstered with her needlepoint work. The Hunzinger recliner on the right was bought at auction with only the frame intact. Cass researched original designs at museums, then sketched out a dragon-and-flower motif similar to original coverings on similar Hunzinger chairs. It took her two years to sketch, paint, and stitch the canvas, which was then applied to a golden topaz Scalamandré velvet, "Bravura." A similar process for the chair on the left resulted in a petit point canvas in a tapestry design. Cass used more than sixty colors throughout the back and seat canvases. A Scalamandré silk in slate blue was used for the button-tufted chair seat.

An Aesthetic Interior for Antiques Collectors

WESTCHESTER COUNTY

This substantial home in New York's Westchester County was bought just five years ago by the current owners. Built by the well-known architect Mott B. Schmidt at the turn of the twentieth century, it features generous spaces that, however, the owners wished to personalize with soft furnishings that would complement their collection of mid-nineteenth-century Aesthetic movement antiques.

Cass began with the entry hall, designing a lambrequin and drapes for the front window. Scalamandré "Monarque"—a cream-based lampas with tulips of light blue, yellow and orange, dotted by embroidered fans of metallic gold thread—was selected. Once the fabric was chosen, Cass was then able to extend the colors throughout the entire foyer. The lambrequin was highlighted with "Tulip" braid and double-tassel tiebacks in sunrise yellow, sunset orange and sky blue, and hand quilted in gold metallic thread to emphasize the gold fan design throughout the brocade-like lampas. A golden maize silk balloon curtain was added underneath and was flanked by embroidered Elitis turquoise silk shantung drapes.

ABOVE A detail of the lambrequin's "Monarque" lampas of multicolored tulips shows the intricate quilting and rich colors of the design. A golden silk balloon curtain peeks out from underneath.

LEFT Cass hand stitched an intricate silk runner for the antique Italian hall table using a combination of seven Scalamandré silks and trims. "Chinese Disc" damask in coral and sky colors and "Penelope" lampas in coral and beige were used, accented with "Shirred Stripe" in Etruscan red and cream, along with a variety of Scalamandré trims and tassels.

FACING The gracious entry hall is anchored at one end by an elaborate window treatment. The lambrequin was constructed from Scalamandré's "Monarque" lampas, which Cass then hand quilted in gold metallic thread as an accent. Warm and cheerful colors were used in the custom Scalamandré trims, from sunrise yellow and sunset orange to sky blue.

ABOVE *Even the wall sconce shades are works of art, hand-sewn in "Patmos" silk taffeta stripes of kiwi, persimmon, and peach, sheered with hand-sewn passementerie and hand-tied silk tassel fringe.*

FACING *The billiard room opens off the entrance hall and is set off by a dramatic arched cornice that combines several fabrics already used in the hallway, including sky blue "Melograno" lampas, coral-and-sky blue "Penelope" lampas, and coral-and-sky blue "Chinese Disc" damask. The half-round settee was reupholstered in the "Melograno" lampas, and braid, bullion, and tricolor cord echo the blue and terra-cotta colors. Hand-tied passementerie buttons in blue, coral, and cream highlight the tufting. The long teardrop pillow is covered in "Penelope" lampas in coral and beige.*

ABOVE *An Egyptian Revival Herter Brothers sofa at the opposite end of the entry hall is upholstered in Scalamandré "Natchez" silk lampas in a ripe peach and cream colorway that complements the window treatment. Cass added strong colors in yellow, green and orange braid along with hand-sewn buttons for more visual interest. Pillows on the sofa are fabricated from materials used in the hall, including "Shirred Stripe," a silk taffeta and repp, and "Monarque" and "Melograno" lampas.*

Once the main window was completed, it led the way for several complementary and companion pieces throughout the foyer, such as an Egyptian Revival Herter Brothers sofa, which was covered in Scalamandré "Natchez" silk damask in cream and ripe peach. An orange, green and yellow flat braid was used, along with custom buttons that Cass made by hand for a more interesting detail. Throw pillows were designed using pieces of the lambrequin cream lampas and matching trims. No detail was too small: hand-sewn sconce lamp shades were designed in Scalamandré "Patmos" silk taffeta stripes of kiwi, persimmon and peach, with silk tassel fringe. Cass designed a table runner for the antique Italian hall table in the persimmon-colored silk damask "Chinese Disc," then added seven Scalamandré trims

and a looped, fringed braid in cream, green and pumpkin. It wasn't long before the entry hall became a favorite conversation area for guests as they admired Cass's handiwork.

Cass continued her work to the opposite end of the entry, which opens into the billiard room. An elaborate valance was designed for the doorway using Scalamandré's "Melograno" lampas in turquoise blue, coupled with coral "Penelope" lampas and coral "Chinese Disc" damask—all of which had been used elsewhere in the foyer, thus helping to tie the space together. The overall effect is a stunning yet complementary treatment. A small, half-round settee was also reupholstered with Scalamandré "Melograno" lampas in variegated turquoise blue.

Colors of garnet, red and turquoise seemed the perfect hues for the living room, accenting the owners' collection of English art pottery. An overstuffed, but very dilapidated, Victorian Turkish chair was rescued and restored with Scalamandré "Osborne" silk-face velvet, set off by elaborate tassel fringe bullion in turquoise, cream and cappuccino taupe. A delicate Scalamandré cream silk damask was used on the lampshade, highlighted by Austrian crystal beads that Cass sewed on by hand for extra sparkle. Warm and inviting, the room virtually glows with the rich colors and designs.

The library was designed in soothing colors of tea rose pink, evergreen and topaz. Antique furniture was again restored, including an ebonized Hunzinger chair for which Cass hand painted and then stitched needlepoint coverings, finally finishing it with a Scalamandré slate silk. The owner bought another Hunzinger chair at auction—a rocker without any material—and Cass designed and hand stitched the needlepoint upholstery for it as well, the whole project taking her two years! 🍎

A pair of brushed-metallic gold Aesthetic side chairs in the living room against the Oriental carpet. Cass's custom-designed and hand-stitched petit point chair seats are accented around the borders by Scalamandré turquoise-and-coral shirred silk. It took six months to complete the petit point for each chair.

LEFT *The living room is furnished in tones of garnet, red and turquoise to accent the owners' collection of Aesthetic movement English art pottery. The Turkish chair, found at auction, was dilapidated and required complete restoration. A lush Scalamandré "Osborne" silk velvet in a peacock color was selected and accented with substantial bullion tassel fringe in turquoise, cream and cappuccino taupe, then finished with a rouched self-edging.*

ABOVE *Even the lamp shades are works of art. Cass hand strung Austrian crystal beads in garnet, turquoise, amber and aurora borealis to accent the Scalamandré cream silk damask selected for the lamp shade cover. Cass offers that her lamp shades are one of her most popular accessories.*

OVERLEAF *A flagstone terrace overlooks the gardens and the Hudson River. Scalamandré's Island Cloth Collection was used to cover the furniture in a combination of black-and-white "Swirl" and black-and-white "Polka Dot" for a striking effect.*

The family's golden lab Honey relaxes by the pool. Outdoor fabrics from the Island Cloth collection were used on the furniture, with a colorful combination of lime and white "Galapagos" woven jacquard, "Antigua" plaid in lime and white, and "Polka Dot," also in lime and white.

Colorful Country Cottage

COLORADO

Cass Daley's own cottage in Colorado reflects her love of color and design. Although she has had numerous opportunities to use her handiwork in large Colorado mountain lodges, when she purchased this cozy cottage, she was able to highlight her skills in a smaller setting. Cass enclosed the one-car garage along one side of the house and converted it into a family den. Even though the entire room is only 200 square feet, she decided to paint the walls a bright sunset-geranium orange to give it warmth. An arched gas fireplace was added, more for ambience than heat, and surrounded with river rock. Knotty-pine wainscoting was installed, along with hickory flooring, to complete the rustic look.

More than forty Scalamandré fabrics and trims were used in this room, so Cass chose a walnut-stained bungalow-style wicker chair to tone down the brightness. "Chinoiserie Exotique" in cotton, trimmed with braid with wooden ball and fringe, was used on the windows for a colorful, homespun look. Cass built an ottoman and covered it with Scalamandré "Persian" cotton, a paisley leaf pattern, trimming it in persimmon tassel fringe for even more color. Antique coral Bakelite buttons give the tufting added detail.

Cass chose cheerful and colorful fabrics and designs for her little girl's room. She hand painted nursery-rhyme characters on the walls, making the ten-foot-square room a cozy playhouse. Thirteen Scalamandré fabrics were used, chosen for their bright and whimsical designs. Cass made a duvet cover from seven different Scalamandré cottons. An antique wicker chair was reupholstered in a maize union cloth and trimmed with Scalamandré's red, sky, green and cream braid. A small Humpty Dumpty lamp, found at a tag sale for five dollars, was dressed up with a Scalamandré cream silk shade; even Humpty's neck bow is a Scalamandré silk ribbon. 🍎

Designed from a former garage, the warm and cozy den has a wide window seat and arched, river rock fireplace. Scalamandré "Shirred Stripe" in Etruscan red and cream was used for the window valance. Pillows are made of pat-terns including "Under the Ice" and "Foret," appropriately rustic themes. For the child's rocker, Cass hand stitched the small silk plaid pillows, which are trimmed in "Mayfair" silk plaid.

ABOVE *Cass's pillows are beautifully detailed on front and back. Here a collection of some of her most recent creations include fish swimming across the sea in sky blue "Under the Ice," charmingly accented with glass fish buttons; "Mayfair Plaid" silk taffeta in the lower left corner; a hand-embroidered needlepoint cushion in an original design; and in the upper left, the back of a cushion in "Belgravia Trellis" lampas, showing how Cass uses antique Bakelite buttons as accents.*

LEFT *The same cushions as above, now turned around, look completely different. A hand-embroidered version of a large fish swimming across the back of "Under the Ice," "Chinoise Exotique" in ecru graces the front of the "Belgravia Trellis" lampas pillow, "Shirred Stripe" in sky and cream backs the "Mayfair Plaid" silk taffeta, and rich brass antique buttons accent the back of the hand-embroidered cushion.*

FACING *The other side of the fireplace is a cozy spot for reading or needle pointing. Here Cass's work in progress is a needlepoint pillow in "Under the Ice." Walls are painted a bright sunset geranium for a warm and intimate feeling. The wicker chair next to the fireplace is covered in coral "Shimmer Silk" and "Penelope" lampas. Cass designed and built the ottoman, covering it in "Persian" and even using antique Bakelite buttons inside the tufts.*

BELOW *"Foret," a figured cotton chenile in 100 percent cotton velvet in forest red is used for this pillow, accented with a multicolored Scalamandré looped fringe.*

FACING *A detail of the wicker chair next to the fireplace upholstered in warm coral colors of "Shimmer Silk" and "Penelope" lampas, accented with Scalamandré looped fringe.*

FACING *A detail of the colorful ottoman that Cass designed and built, covered in "Persian" ecru and trimmed with an assortment of Scalamandré trims. The tufts have antique Bakelite buttons inside.*

RIGHT *A wrought-iron chandelier lights the small dining room off the kitchen, its shades covered in "Shirred Stripe" in Naples yellow. The French doors are covered with flat Roman shades in "Arcadia," a multicolored-on-cream union cloth, in warm yellow tones.*

BELOW *Each shade was handsewn by Cass in "Shirred Stripe" with biased ribbing.*

FACING *Cass's daughter's room is a sunny yellow, accented by hand-painted nursery rhyme characters. The antique wicker chair was reupholstered in maize union cloth, highlighted by Scalamandré braid in red, sky, green and cream. The duvet cover is a cheerful mix of seven Scalamandré cottons. Even the Humpty Dumpty lamp, found at a tag sale for $5, is covered with Scalamandré silk.*

LEFT   *Detail of the intricate and colorful duvet cover uses a mélange of Scalamandré cottons from yellow-and-blue "Mayfair Plaid" to pink-and-lemon "Floreale" and two colorways of "Jour de Juin."*

FACING   *The Humpty Dumpty lampshade is covered in a Scalamandré silk and trimmed with Scalamandré pastel fringe and braid.*

A designer for more than twenty-five years, Melinda's career has included a wide range of work, from small business design to wardrobe consultation to home interiors. Melinda strives to build long-term relationships with her clients, finding that successful relationships are essential to ensure that her clients receive what they want and thus find the hidden beauty and warmth in their homes.

Melinda's design philosophy is simple: give everyone a little more than they expect. Updating existing pieces with new upholstery and exuberant colors, she helps her clients realize more expensive treatments than they thought they could originally afford.

A perfect example of Melinda's successful relationships with her clients is the story of a couple living in a turn-of-the-twentieth-century Arts and Crafts home on Seattle's Queen Anne Hill. What began as a simple request for a dining room table has turned into a long-lasting relationship, helping make a vintage home one that is comfortable, inviting, and exciting with color, pattern, and a dash of quirkiness. Melinda has shopped with her clients in Europe and the States, looking for just the right furnishings and accents. And Melinda's skills in communication and understanding her clients' needs have made this an enjoyable process for them both.

Vibrant Craftsman Bungalow

SEATTLE

FACING *The bungalow's simple parlor comes alive with warmth and color. Walls are covered in sunny yellow stripes, and the windows are brightened with Scalamandré's cotton "Duchessa" in colors of green and brick on beige, repeated in pillows for the chairs. A pair of Scalamandré "Melrose" chairs, covered in the warm stripes of the cotton "Bella Rigoletta" in umber and ochre sits in front of the window, while a Scalamandré wing chair rests in the corner, covered in the soft green paisley "Gunga Din." Original built-in bookcases were wisely kept intact; the glass doors were shirred with Scalamandré's cotton "Fleur Renaissance" for privacy. A pair of matching Scalamandré "Clementine" footstools and a button-tufted "Windsor" ottoman complete the room's décor.*

RIGHT *The cheerful flowers of "Duchessa" form a perfect valance for the small window above the bookcases, accented with elegant "Duchessa" fringe.*

ABOVE *Even the shades for the overhead chandelier are covered with Scalamandré fabric. Melinda chose the candy cane colors of the contemporary jacquard "Parfait," accented with a small cuff of "Powers Court" strie taffeta silk in jade green for a bright and cheerful effect.*

FACING *The footstools are exuberantly covered with the colorful cut-velvet "Pitti" and accented with silk "Duchessa Fringe" and large pendants of "Hampton Court" mold fringe. This is the homeowner's favorite spot to kick off her shoes and relax!*

Kent Kiesey's parents ran a successful decorating and furniture business in the Midwest, so he was exposed to interior design at an early age. His parents would sometimes ask Kent to help, at first having him just dust the furniture but eventually encouraging his creativity through designing window displays. After graduating from college with a degree in interior design, his first job was at Marshall Field's in Chicago. Kent soon learned all the practical aspects of the trade, from meeting with clients to shopping and maintaining personal involvement in each order. Kent was asked to design a model home, "Trend House," in the store in 1979; it remained open for one year and was so successful that he began receiving design jobs from clients throughout the Chicago area, many of whom he still keeps in contact with today.

After sixteen years, Kent left Marshall Field's to open his own design business. He strives to do all of his own shopping and ordering, and prides himself on maintaining close, personal relationships with his clients. Kent feels it is important to always listen to his clients to determine their wants and needs, and then interpret them with classic, timeless designs.

English Regency Contemporary

CHICAGO

Kent's clients requested that their dining room and living room coordinate in a contemporary English Regency style. While everything needed to be basic, the furnishings and décor also needed to be splendid. Kent accomplished this look by using a cool and clear two-color palette of green and white. Bare wood floors laid in herringbone pattern remained simple yet rich. Fabrics for both rooms were chosen for their luxuriousness, with elegant details such as silk fringe on the pillows and furniture and jade fringe on the curtains. 🍂

RIGHT *The living room is light and airy in shades of white and pale green. "Jade" trim is repeated on the curtains in the room. The sofa is covered in Scalamandré "Chinoiserie" damask, while Scalamandré trim was used for the rosettes and pillows.*

OVERLEAF *Symmetrical and elegant, the dining room is centered on an ebonized Regency-style table and chairs. White walls and pale green curtains create a cool look.*

ABOVE *Maisy, the family's Tibetan terrier, steals a moment on an English Regency–style hall bench, which is trimmed in Scalamandré silk cording and tassels.*

FACING, ABOVE *Scalamandré silk trim subtly accents the "Chinoiserie" covering on the sofa pillows.*

FACING, BELOW *Louis XVI fauteuils in the living room have contrasting backs for accent and are enhanced with Scalamandré silk trim.*

Chinoiserie Red-and-White Toile

CHICAGO

Kent's own bedroom was designed around his favorite color—red. He wanted a warm and intimate but slightly lively look. Scalamandré "Pillement Toile" linen, which is based on a 1785 French pattern, was used to cover the walls. A spirited design in the style of Jean Pillement, it features an elegantly dressed Chinaman shaded by a parasol, set against a backdrop of huge blooms and rococo scrolls. Kent carried the Oriental theme onto the ceiling, designing a plaster ceiling after that of the Richardson House in Savannah, with corner "pedantries" appearing as reversed parasols.

ABOVE *A small sofa in the bedroom is also covered in "Pillement Toile" and accented with a robust red Scalamandré bullion fringe. A collection of pillows made from vintage fabrics and Scalamandré "Shirred Stripe" was used for the round pillows.*

RIGHT *Bright and cheerful, Kent's bedroom walls have been lined with felt and covered in Scalamandré's linen "Pillement Toile." The plaster ceiling treatment was handmade by a local plasterer, based on a similar ceiling in the historic Richardson House in Savannah. A leopard rug provides a counterbalance to the red and white.*

Neoclassical Study in Gold

CHICAGO

The owners of this Chicago brownstone wanted an elegant study on their top floor, continuing the feeling found in the rest of their home. Collectors of antiques, the owners have purchased their furniture on frequent trips to France and England. Kent reconditioned a pair of French Empire chairs or sofa, covering them in Scalamandré "Louis XVI" silk, and pillows were also made in coordinating Scalamandré damasks. The walls of the study were painted in a mottled greenish gold texture and then highlighted with a high-gloss lacquer, transforming the entire room into a gilded jewel box. A recessed ceiling dome was installed to add to the classic look. Olive green velvet curtains, trimmed in Scalamandré bullion fringe, were draped in a manner to let the light stream in.

LEFT   *A French Empire dark green and gilded bench is handsomely upholstered in Scalamandré "Pompeian Memories" for a Napoleonic look.*

ABOVE   *Draped curtains let in plenty of light. The olive green, tasseled, cut fringe is Scalamandré, as well as the coordinating tiebacks.*

FACING   *The gold study glistens like a jewel box with lacquered gold walls and French Empire furniture covered in the sunny yellow tones of Scalamandré "Louis XVI" silk.*

Nineteenth-Century Winter Reading Room

CHICAGO

A winter reading room was designed by Kent for this nineteenth-century Chicago brownstone. The clients requested dark colors, and there needed to be sufficient seating to comfortably accommodate six people for conversation. Deep, rich reds and rusts were chosen to make the room warm and inviting.

The owners are enamored of all things Oriental, and thus the room's wood trim and bookcases were constructed in maple, then faux painted in a bamboo pattern that would have been quite appropriate for the home as the late-nineteenth-century Anglo-Japanese craze was sweeping across the country when the home was being built in 1881. Scalamandré "Fusina Ceiling" was installed and "Pillement Toile" was used to accent a staircase leading upstairs. "Villa Farnese," a Colony figured velvet for Scalamandré, covers a French loveseat and pillows, for a warm, wintry look. 🍎

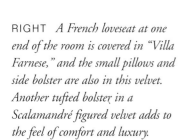

RIGHT *A French loveseat at one end of the room is covered in "Villa Farnese," and the small pillows and side bolster are also in this velvet. Another tufted bolster in a Scalamandré figured velvet adds to the feel of comfort and luxury.*

FACING *The warm tones of the winter reading room are accented by Scalamandré "Fusina Ceiling" paper. Deep, rich reds and rusts make this a room that invites houseguests to curl up with a good book on a sofa. Scalamandré "Portofino" sheers hang between the velvet curtains on the window.*

John Rolland has been an interior designer based in Philadelphia for fifteen years, specializing in sophisticated English- and French-inspired interiors. John enjoys combining fine antiques with the best available classic fabrics and furnishings.

Classic Continental Elegance

RITTENHOUSE SQUARE

Two years ago, when John learned of an apartment for sale in the Barclay, one of Philadelphia's most prestigious prewar buildings overlooking Rittenhouse Square, he did not hesitate to purchase it for himself. Built in 1929 as the finest hotel in Philadelphia, the Barclay had always been operated as a residential hotel as well as guest lodging. But changing times had not been kind to the grand building, and it had been allowed to fall into such a state of disrepair that plans were made to have it closed and demolished. When a local developer stepped in and bought the neglected hotel in 2000, saving it from the wrecking ball, a multimillion-dollar restoration was put in motion that would return the building and its apartments to their former grandeur.

The entrance foyer is papered in a colorful combination of Scalamandré "Fusina Ceiling" in gold, green and wine, and a Regency-style wallpaper. An English Chippendale console supports Rose Canton ginger jars and is flanked by Regency chairs, c. 1820. A late-Georgian mirror rests above. The ceiling was kept low to enhance the transition from the foyer to the main parlor.

A detail of the foyer showing the c. 1790 water-gilt late Georgian mirror that echoes the patterns and colors of the ceiling and wallpapers.

ABOVE *An English Regency satinwood bench with hand-painted flowers, c. 1820, rests along an opposite wall in the foyer. Its seat is covered in Scalamandré "Shirred Stripe" in persimmon and brown, accented with silk cording. A pillow in Scalamandré "Brompton Plaid" in rose and cream, accented with silk tassel fringe, picks up the colors of the bench perfectly.*

LEFT *Ebonized and gilded English Regency armchairs in the foyer are upholstered in "Ascot" silk taffeta, accented with dark green silk cording and button tufts.*

When John bought his apartment (actually, four hotel rooms) it was in a sorry state, with peeling wallpaper and in need of total restoration. But John was undeterred, and impressed by the apartment's spaciousness and large windows overlooking Rittenhouse Square, he quickly went to work, keeping the original configuration of the rooms but replacing and updating the remainder of the apartment. It now sparkles as an elegant testimonial to John's restoration and decorating skills. He has skillfully combined English Regency and Chippendale antiques with fine Scalamandré fabrics and wallpapers for a timeless and elegant look.

LEFT *A Rose Medallion table lamp in the parlor is a custom-made shade in Scalamandré "Gossamer" silk plaid with a silk fringe. The lamp rests on a Regency satinwood vitrine table holding some of John's collection of eighteenth-century English Bilstone boxes meant to hold snuff, patches (to cover smallpox scars) or candies.*

FACING *The main parlor has been returned to its prewar elegance. The walls have been upholstered in the gold, tone-off-tone cotton damask. Panels are trimmed with gold silk gimp. The Duke of Bridgewater, the Lord Mayor of London in 1820, strikes a commanding pose over the sofa, which is upholstered in the damask, as well, with gold silk cording and bullion fringe. A pair of Louis XV armchairs, their backs upholstered in the yellow damask and still maintaining their original gilt finish, flank the sofa. A Regency tole tray on a painted bamboo stand serves as a coffee table, set with c. 1770 Bilstone enameled candlesticks and a Rose Medallion tea set. Note the large Rose Medallion lamp that has a custom shade in Scalamandré "Shirred Stripe." A French Aubusson carpet, c. 1820, anchors the room.*

FACING *The warm and inviting den is paneled and covered in strie-pattern wallpaper. The sofa is upholstered in Scalamandré "Elenora" antique velvet in dark blue, and is accented with a hand-painted pillow bearing a spaniel. Hand-colored, antique botanical prints of parrots are grouped on the wall above the sofa. The curtains are Scalamandré "Baroque Floral" printed linen, as are two flanking overstuffed chairs. An ottoman was upholstered in a Scalamandré novelty jacquard in rust and beige.*

ABOVE *The master bath is decorated in shades of pale blues, with hand-painted Chinese silk wallpaper and a blue celeste marble console. A pair of eighteenth-century Bilstone candlesticks have been converted into lamps, their shades covered in Scalamandré "Tipperary" silk stripe in blue and white, with silk tassel fringe.*

Nancy Serafini loves renovation. So much so, in fact, that she specializes in designing and restoring homes from the ground up, often beginning with the basic layout and construction. The award-winning designer has operated her own business since the age of twenty-five, participating in projects from historic home restorations to private interiors, where she likes to achieve an English country look with an eclectic mix of antique and modern furnishings. Nancy enjoys the process of discovery and finds that by uncovering and addressing problems initially, she is able to build the foundation for a successful design. Nancy's own Boston Back Bay apartment best exemplifies her considerable talents.

Brahmin Traditional

BOSTON'S BACK BAY

Nancy Serafini and her husband were not thinking about moving from their comfortable Wellesley, Massachusetts, home. They had lived there for more than twenty years while raising their two children. But Nancy, an interior designer who heads her own successful design company, Homeworks, visited a large prewar apartment on Boston's Back Bay one afternoon in 1999 with her husband, and it was love at first sight for them both. The 3,400-square-foot apartment, comprising the entire seventh floor of a 1929 building, had been virtually untouched for over twenty-five years. Original walnut paneling and window seats were still intact in the living room, which featured stunning views of the Charles River and Cambridge. The apartment was bathed in light, with windows on all sides, and this, along with the ample-sized rooms, convinced Nancy and her husband to purchase the apartment after just one visit.

Of course, major structural work was required, from rewiring and replumbing to reconfiguring the rooms to create a master suite, a den and a high-tech galley kitchen. But as Nancy points out, "the bones were right." Taking her cue from the original paneling in the living room, Nancy created a warm palette of vibrant golds and rich reds, accented with silk taffeta curtains in Scalamandré "Napoli's" silk stripe. A warm combination of overstuffed chairs and whimsical antiques created a room that is inviting and comfortable.

PREVIOUS OVERLEAF *The living room extends across the entire front of the apartment and features beautiful views of the Charles River. Original walnut paneling provided the inspiration for the room's burnished tones of golds and reds. Curtains in Scalamandré "Napoli's" silk stripe tie it all together. Scalamandré's Knightsbridge sofa in a muted green "Paddington" velvet rests along one end of the twenty-six-foot-long room and holds a collection of pillows.*

FACING *A window seat overlooks the Charles River. A balloon shade in Scalamandré "Napoli's" striped silk warms the area. An antique English beaded pillow and Victorian accessories, such as a Gothic brass-and-velvet picture frame and a large needlepoint embroidery of a parrot on the wall, add to the period décor.*

RIGHT *A Windsor Ottoman from Scalamandré is covered in "Marly," a figured linen-faced velvet, and comes in handy as an extra table. The carpet is Mark Inc.'s "Amandari Cinnabar."*

BELOW *A sofa pillow in plaid silk complements the rich red- and-gold "Napoli's" striped curtain. The tiebacks are just the right accent.*

ABOVE   *A vintage Swedish hand-painted plate rail holds
some of Nancy's collection of Luneville china that is nicely
accented by "Minton Rose" plaid used as wallpaper.*

FACING   *The powder room was designed around the
Victorian marble commode found while antiquing in
Connecticut. Scalamandré "Minton Rose" plaid was chosen
for the walls, with balloon shades in the companion fabric.*

Decorating, Meredith Moriarty likes to say, is not a life-threatening process. An interior designer in the Chicago area for twenty-two years, Meredith likes to make decorating pleasurable for everyone. She admits that she plays the roles of decorator, director, producer, philosopher and psychologist as she works with her clients to make important decisions based on memo samples of fabrics and carpets, pictures of furniture and renderings of window treatments. Meredith emphasizes that a decorator is only as good as the quality of the suppliers and the skills of the workrooms engaged. The goal for each project, she reminds us, is to ensure that the client has an enjoyable experience, which, in turn, helps guarantee that they will love their home when everything is finished and installed.

Georgian Classicism

CHICAGO

Meredith's clients for this project, a young couple with active children, built a 7,500-square-foot home in the north Chicago suburbs in a classic Georgian style. Red, blue and yellow are the clients' favorite colors, so Meredith designed their home with variations on this basic palette.

Scalamandré's sunny "Jour de Juin" silk was used for the master suite, complemented with the colorful striped silk "Candy." Meredith had a pair of bedside commodes hand painted in "Jour de Juin" for amusing accents, and the same pattern was continued in the master bath as cotton shades.

Downstairs, the living room was designed around a formal Georgian medallion carpet that was custom made for the room. Walls were glazed a soft yellow, and classic furniture was added, including an English Knoll sofa upholstered in a coral-, blue- and milk-striped silk lampas from Scalamandré, "Monroe Arabesque." Slippered chairs were upholstered with a Scalamandré silk lampas, "Monroe Bee," in the same colorway to continue the classic and elegant look.

A hand-painted Julia Gray desk in the hall outside the master bedroom is accented with a chair upholstered in "Jour de Juin" and "Candy" silks.

The master bedroom is a cheerful spot throughout the day. Walls are glazed in sunny yellow, and Scalamandré "Jour de Juin" silk provides the perfect upholstery for the Julia Gray four-poster bed. Even the commodes are hand painted in the "Jour de Juin" pattern of intricate flowers and insects. Colorful Scalamandré "Candy" silk is used as an attractive accent on the duvet and an upholstered side chair and ottoman. A simple green-and-white lattice-patterned carpet is the anchor.

FACING *The Julia Gray commode is covered with flowers and tiny insects hand painted in Scalamandré's "Jour de Juin" design.*

RIGHT *Detail of the duvet showing the pleasing contrast of the delicate stripes of "Candy" silk with the broader bands of the pillow covers.*

LEFT *A rainbow of colors in "Candy" silk sparkles on the side chair and ottoman.*

FACING *The theme of flowers and insects is carried into the master bath, where "Jour de Juin" in cotton is used for window shades and an upholstered bench.*

The dining room was also designed around a custom-made carpet with a central medallion, carefully positioned in front of the fireplace in the center of the room. Two round dining tables, each seating up to eight, were chosen to add a more intimate ambiance to gatherings. Scalamandré's colorful "Le Cirque" silk, used as upholstery for the dining room chairs, coordinated perfectly with the brightly colored red-yellow-and-blue silk taffeta curtains.

The husband was not forgotten in the home's design: a large screened porch at the back of the house was furnished in Scalamandré's whimsical printed union cloth "Under the Ice" and wicker furniture, and is now his favorite spot for retiring after dinner to enjoy a good cigar. ❧

FACING *Rich red glazed walls set off the dining room, which is made more intimate by two round mahogany tables on either side of the fireplace. Chairs around each table are upholstered in Scalamandré's colorful "Le Cirque" silk. The carpet was custom designed and centered in the room. Plate rails along the back wall show off the owner's antique porcelain plate collection.*

RIGHT *Strong reds, yellows and blues are repeated in the silk taffeta curtains, which were custom made in wide stripes. The bright colors are echoed in the chair seats, which are covered with "Le Cirque" silk.*

FACING *Detail of the slippered side chair upholstered in "Monroe Bee," showing a boxed pleat beautifully accented with a complementary tassel and cord.*

ABOVE *Bolsters for the Knoll sofa are also in "Monroe Arabesque," with end buttons of complementary cording.*

OVERLEAF *Comfortable wicker furniture upholstered in Scalamandré's printed union cloth "Under the Ice" makes the screened sun porch the husband's favorite retreat for an after-dinner cigar. A small hooked rug of fish found in Vermont is just the right accent.*

Carol Knott didn't start out to be a designer. In fact, she completed nearly all of her course work for pre-med studies at Northwestern University before deciding to pursue her other true interest—interior design—graduating with a degree in art. Carol had been fascinated with interiors as long as she could remember. One of her favorite stories is when, at the age of eight, her mother sent her to the furniture store by herself to choose the family's new dining room table.

Following college, Carol worked for several years for another designer and then established her own business, specializing in residential interiors. Carol points out that being an interior designer is much like being a physician, as both are professions in which one works intimately with people in a helping role. In business now for nearly forty years, Carol has had the pleasure of designing interiors for generations of families—parents, children and grandchildren—often becoming a beloved member of their extended families. Her continuing success is based on her open and trusting relationships.

Carol has no plans to retire, she laughs, as she continues to learn every day and feels lucky to have a career that is so enjoyable. We will visit two of Carol's projects in the Chicago area: the first a warm and masculine library for a young family, and the second a magical little girl's room and a classic living room filled with color in the same home.

Neoclassical Library

CHICAGO

The soft golden yellow house with green shutters sets a tone of welcome and classic appeal. The owners, a young couple with two children, wanted a library that could be a retreat for both of them—especially the husband, who often works at home. The room began with an antique desk found in New Orleans that was large and yet sophisticated, a perfect fit for the wide bay window. A desk chair was upholstered in Scalamandré "Edwin's Covey," a

The warm and inviting library features deeply glazed, rich red walls and furnishings in an autumn palette of golds, greens and reds. The curtains are in Scalamandré "Belgravia" lampas, as is the skirted table. An ottoman was constructed and covered with "Arthur" brocatelle in warm tones of ochre and beige. Charlie, the family's Shih Tzu puppy, is allowed on the leather sofa when he is good. The library is a favorite spot for the husband to work at the desk or smoke a cigar.

hand-printed union cloth with a sporting motif of quail and flowers as a traditional accent. An armoire to the right of the desk conceals the computer.

A rug was chosen to complement the greens and rusty reds of the room, and also to accent the family's Shih Tzu puppy, Charlie, who is soft tan and golden brown: when Charlie is good, he is allowed on the soft, brown leather sofa. An ottoman was covered in Scalamandré "Arthur" brocatelle in ochre and beige and doubles as a sofa table. A combination of pillows includes one in "Shirred Stripe" taffeta and repp trimmed with silk "Newport" tassel fringe in ivory, old gold, buttercup and dark cardinal; another in "Duca Di Mantova" lampas; and a third in the hand-printed velvet paisley "Highland Fling."

Opulent draperies in the reds and golds of Scalamandré's lampas "Belgravia," complete with swags and tiebacks, add a sophisticated touch and harmonize perfectly with the deep, rich reds of the glazed walls. A table skirted in "Belgravia" provides a colorful accent in the corner. A fireplace at the opposite end of the room makes this a place for work, quiet talk, or just a gathering spot for the guys and a good cigar. ✍

FACING *Draperies are made of Scalamandré's lampas "Belgravia" in warm autumn colors of oro scuro (antique gold). "Muriel" silk tassel fringe in a soft gold, red and cream sets off the lampas. Note the lovely tiebacks, Scalamandré's "Double Duchessa" with exotic yellow-jade medallions.*

ABOVE *A pair of pillows—the first in "Shirred Stripe" taffeta and repp in antique gold, brick and cream trimmed with multicolored "Newport" tassel fringe, and the second in Gothic "Duca Di Mantova" cotton lampas—are perfect complements for the rich tones of the leather sofa.*

ABOVE   *"Highland Fling" paisley-printed velvet, accented with "Duchessa" silk tassel fringe, makes a warm pillow for the back of a comfy leather armchair.*

FACING   *A desk chair was upholstered in "Edwin's Covey," a hand-printed Scalamandré union cloth, for a sporting accent. The handsome, burled walnut desk was found in New Orleans and fits perfectly in the bay window.*

A Little Girl's Whimsical Wonderland

CHICAGO

Carol's library clients introduced her to good friends of theirs, and it wasn't long before Carol was asked to help them refurbish their 1920s traditional redbrick Colonial Revival home.

Carol began upstairs, designing an enchanted room for their six-year-old daughter. The child loves pink and Carol was thrilled to find Scalamandré's rosy pink cotton toile "Jeanette sur la Plage," which features Victorian children playing by the sea. For the Gustavian bed, the footboard and headboard are upholstered in the cheerful toile, and a duvet cover from the toile is ruffled and trimmed with a bias edge of silk "Tipperary Check."

Window treatments were also constructed from "Jeanette sur la Plage." A pair of tabourets at the foot of the bed were covered in Scalamandré's silk moiré taffeta "Vicomte" in plum. A comfortable, tufted Elizabeth Chair and Caitlin Ottoman from Scalamandré were added to the side of the bed, upholstered in the hand-printed silk "Caprice des Dames" in a rose-and-cream colorway. An area rug in pink and white was chosen, trimmed all around with Scalamandré's silk fringe "Fragonard" as a special touch.

A local muralist was engaged to paint a whimsical scene of sand castles and bunnies on the wall opposite the bed, inspired by "Jeanette sur la Plage." The artist also painted trompe l'oeil drapery around the other walls, enveloping the room in swaths of curtains, and added a corona above the headboard in the toile design. The room has become a magical retreat for the daughter and her friends. ❧

Pink, the little girl's favorite color, was used to design this enchanting room. Scalamandré's playful cotton toile "Jeanette sur la Plage" in a rosy pink was selected for the draperies, duvet, and footboard and headboard upholstery. Tabourets in Scalamandré "Vicomte" silk moiré taffeta in plum rest at the foot of the bed. Scalamandré's Elizabeth Chair and Caitlin Ottoman, upholstered in the hand-printed silk "Caprice des Dames," were placed bedside. A pillow in "Decatur Stripe" rests on the chair. A soft pink-and-white area carpet, makes a fine flooring for girls at play.

FACING An elaborately skirted table rests in front of the hand-painted mural. Pale green-and-white "Bonnie Plaid" in cotton and silk was used for the skirt, accented by "Hampton Court" open-scroll braid in pink, red and green with the matching mold fringe. "Ingrid," a fancy jacquard in pinks and cream, was used for the scalloped topper that is edged in "Tulip" braid with a corded center in pink, red, cream and green. The table lamp was found in Paris.

ABOVE A bed canopy was constructed from Scalamandré "Jolie Chapeau" cotton voile sheers, which feature embroidered gnats buzzing across the fabric. The curtains are trimmed with a pink-and-cream tape and tied back with a rosette of Scalamandré's silk "Tipperary Check."

LEFT Even the doll's chair is upholstered in Scalamandré—"Dauphine," a red-on-taupe strie lampas. Note the "Fragonard" silk fringe rug border. The mural provides a whimsical backdrop.

A Warm Traditional Parlor

NORTH CHICAGO

After finishing their little girl's room, the clients turned to their parlor. The 1920s traditional redbrick is located on three acres in north Chicago. The clients lived in the house with little furniture for nearly two years before deciding on the refurbishing scheme. While a two-story addition to the back of the house has been planned to double its size, the living room was kept in its original location.

The client needed everything, so Carol began from the ground up in the living room, moving a doorway and adding a graceful mantel painted in faux marble. Walls were covered in a strong, luminous, yellow English wallpaper. A large grand piano had to stay, and furniture was thus fitted around it. An overstuffed sofa provided the color scheme, upholstered in Scalamandré "Mercante Di Venezia Rigatto" multicolored, striped damask. Elaborate draperies in Scalamandré "La Perouse" antique gold lampas puddle around the floor-to-ceiling windows, accented with "Edward's" scalloped silk tassel fringe in old gold, fern and wine. A pair of tufted chairs with turned walnut legs are covered in Scalamandré's soft gold silk velvet "De Medico" and provide comfortable seating, along with a collection of footstools and benches covered in Scalamandré fabrics.

The overall room now glows in warm and sunny tones and is the wife's favorite spot to relax in the evenings after a long day, with a cup of tea and her favorite decorating books. ✺

LEFT *Comfortable seating is grouped around the faux-marble-painted fireplace, which features real Irish green marble on the hearth and surround. The tufted chairs are covered in Scalamandré's gold silk velvet "De Medico," and the large, soft ottoman wears "Villa Farnese" figured velvet. Tassel-fringed pillows in "San Piero," a cut and voided striped velvet, rest on the upholstered chairs. A French bergere is covered on its back and sides with Scalamandré's silk lampas "Monroe Bee" in celadon, putty and milk.*

RIGHT *A charming carpet footstool is covered in Scalamandré's "San Piero" in cut velvet stripes of rubies on gold, coral and charcoal. Notice the heavy bullion fringe "Fleurival" that anchors the base of the sofa.*

LEFT *Both children and adults enjoy the footstools. Gathered together, they include a low Berlin footstool on the right covered in "Maxim," a cotton gros point; a taller Napoli bench behind, covered in the greens and golds of the contemporary jacquard "Parfait"; a large, round ottoman in the figured velvet "Villa Farnese"; and even a child's chair covered in "Strawberry," a delicate silk liseré.*

BELOW *A colorful assortment of pillows rests on the sofa. Fabrics include Scalamandré's silk taffeta and repp "Shirred Stripe" in antique gold, brick and cream, accented with a striking center tassel and "Newport" silk tassel fringe in ivory, old gold, buttercup and dark cardinal. "San Piero" cut-velvet stripe was used for another pillow with "Rousillon" double trim in garnet, golds and greens. A third pillow in Scalamandré's cut-velvet "Pitti" in rose on gold with "Le Tour" plaited cord in a matching gold completes the colorful grouping.*

FACING *The floor-to-ceiling windows are covered with "La Perouse" lampas, accented by "Edward's" scalloped silk tassel fringe. "Tulip" double-tassel tiebacks in cream, lemon and antique gold hold the draperies in place. A large, skirted table centered in front of the windows is covered with Scalamandré's silk damask "Nashville" in copper and antique gold and holds an antique Rose Medallion lamp and porcelain.*

Betsy Best was raised in the South and attributes her eye for design to the two great influences in her life—her mother and her grandmother. Betsy's grandmother decorated her home in classic taste, with fine antiques purchased in London, and Betsy's mother carried on the tradition. As Betsy recalls, her mother was always looking at floor plans, trying to decide what furniture looked best where, basing her decisions on factors such as windows and lighting. Betsy's mother stressed the importance of first impressions, such as an entrance hall that set the tone for the rest of the house. It's no wonder that Betsy obtained a master's in real estate with a concentration in construction and design. Betsy worked in design at an Atlanta showroom and, since marrying thirteen years ago, has furnished beautiful homes for her family and a few fortunate friends wherever she has lived.

Redbrick Regency

TAMPA

When Betsy's husband's work moved them to Tampa in the fall of 2002, she was elated to find a gracious, redbrick Georgian on a tree-lined, cobblestone street. Built in 1990, it had all the details Betsy was looking for, from extensive moldings and coffered ceilings to a veranda overlooking the backyard pool, and even an upstairs balcony with Chinese Chippendale-style railings.

Betsy used one of her favorite buildings, Brighton Pavilion in England, as her source of inspiration, filling the rooms with English export, Regency-style furnishings and papier-mâché, highlighting the romanticized English vision of Oriental exoticism. Betsy employed tones of reds, blues and golds throughout the rooms downstairs, varying the shades in each room.

The sweeping staircase and elaborate moldings of the entrance hall set a gracious tone for the home. The Regency sofa is upholstered in "Chevalier," a striped jacquard in warm reds and golds. A skirted table used to display some of Betsy's antique Oriental lacquer ware is covered in Scalamandré's cotton damask "Damaschino Bernini." The rug and chandelier are both antiques.

The entrance features a wide, sweeping staircase and sets a gracious tone for the home. A classic nineteenth-century Regency sofa is upholstered in the warm golds and reds of Scalamandré's jacquard striped "Chevalier," while a skirted corner table covered in "Damaschino Bernini" cotton damask in a warm rosso (red) color displays some of Betsy's antique ebonized lacquer ware collection. The inviting living room opens off the entrance hall and is furnished with a colorful collection of furniture upholstered in a warm mix of Scalamandré fabrics. Curtains in "Napoli," a striped silk taffeta in rich chardonnay and burgundy, cover the windows. A wing chair is upholstered in Scalamandré's brocatelle "Reggio" in tones of gold on red and is paired with a mahogany armchair covered in the bold Venetian-red polka dots of Scalamandré "Puntini" damask.

In the dining room, to the left of the entrance hall, the walls are covered in "Shanghai," an exotic hand-printed paper, and accented by gold silk taffeta drapes in "Ascot." Regency-style dining chairs covered with "Napoli" striped silk that was used in the living room help reinforce the connection between the two rooms. Directly behind the entrance hall, a comfortable family room is filled with an assortment of Scalamandré pillows and ottomans. The room is anchored by draperies in the warm mustard tones of Scalamandré's hand-printed cotton "Chinoise Exotique."

A spacious sunroom off the kitchen is enlivened by pillows in the cheerful blues and yellows of "Brompton Plaid," "Le Cirque," and "Le Gingerole."

Outdoors, the veranda and pool chaises are also covered in Scalamandré's outdoor fabrics—"Swirl," "Polka Dot," and "Galapagos"—for a bright summery look. ❧

A close view of the entrance hall sofa reveals its beautiful and classic lines accented by Scalamandré "Chevalier" striped jacquard. Bolsters for the sofa are upholstered in the same fabric.

ABOVE *A wing chair upholstered in Scalamandré's brocatelle "Reggio" coordinates well with the reds and golds of the "Napoli" striped silk curtains. The pillow is covered in the strawberry tones of "Pirouette," a soft chenille polka-dotted jacquard, and trimmed with "Tulip" braid fringe in tomato, gold and olive.*

RIGHT *The warm golds and reds of "Napoli" striped silk taffeta curtains are trimmed with "Duchessa," a silk tassel fringe.*

FACING   *The living room features an assortment of furniture upholstered in colorful Scalamandré materials. The drapes are constructed in a striped silk taffeta, "Napoli." Chairs include a wing chair upholstered in "Reggio" brocatelle in gold on red, and a mahogany armchair playfully covered with the striking polka dots of the damask "Puntini."*

BELOW   *"Puntini" polka dots are a pleasing contrast to "Livia," a cotton-silk blend in Venetian red that covers the Regency chair behind.*

ABOVE *Betsy's antique children's Blue Willow tea set rests among the pillows in the sunroom, which include (from left) a sunny cotton, "Brompton Plaid," an exuberant, French-woven moiré cotton, "Le Cirque," and "Le Gingerole," a hand-printed union cloth.*

FACING *Higgins, the family's soft-coated Wheaten terrier, relaxes in the sunroom that opens off the kitchen. Betsy chose a combination of blue and yellow to make pillows in "Brompton Plaid," "Le Cirque," and "Le Gingerole" for a sunny, cheerful look*

FACING *The family room overlooking the pool at the back of the house is decorated in the rich blues, reds and yellows of the rest of the home. Inspired by Brighton Pavilion in England, Betsy added accessories such as a chinoiserie-style mirror and antique ebonized lacquer ware shelves to hold her Chinese porcelain. A pair of Scalamandré Montauk sofas are upholstered in the cotton taffeta "Strathmore Striae" in strawberry red. Pillows include one in mustard-yellow "Chinoise Exotique," a second in yellow-and-red cotton velvet "Marco Polo" trimmed with persimmon "Trapunto" cotton metalassé, and a third, smaller pillow, in "Calmara," a printed cotton in brightly colored geranium and blue on a smoke blue ground.*

ABOVE *The brightly colored exotic flowers of the printed cotton "Calmara," seen on the ottoman and pillow, coordinate nicely with the blue, red and yellow plaids on Scalamandré's Key Biscayne Chair.*

RIGHT *Detail of "Calmara" pillow, trimmed with "Tulip" braid fringe in wedgwood, gold, and cherry.*

LEFT The dining room is papered in "Shanghai," Betsy's favorite wallpaper, as its chinoiserie scenes are abundant with color and she can use almost any china with it. Curtains are done in Scalamandré's bright gold silk taffeta "Ascot," highlighted with Scalamandré's multicolored Mulberry silk tassel fringe "Follies" in red, egg, royal and green. The Regency-style table is set for dessert with some of Betsy's antique family silver and china. A vintage Heris Oriental carpet defines the dining area.

ABOVE Antique lacquered boxes and an Oriental table lamp echo the exoticism of the mysterious land of Cathay, depicted in "Shanghai," hand-printed paper toile.

FACING   *The kitchen continues the theme of sunny yellow and blue, with Scalamandré's hand-printed, cream-on-blue-and-yellow "Baldwin Bamboo" paper. Betsy's blue-and-white china is perfectly at home in the setting.*

ABOVE   *Chaises around the pool are covered in Scalamandré's lemon-and-off-white contemporary jacquard double-cloth "Swirl"; the pillows are upholstered in the reverse side of "Swirl."*

LEFT   *The veranda across the back of the house, facing the pool, is furnished with wrought-iron chairs and a sofa covered in a variety of Scalamandré's Island Cloth Collection of outdoor fabrics, including (on the sofa) lemon yellow "Polka Dot," blue "Swirl" on the chairs by the sofa, pillows in blue "Galapagos," and the bold stripes of sky-and-off-white "Barbados" on the chairs and ottomans in the foreground.*

JZ Knight is an American legend and world-renowned spiritual teacher who has been an icon for millions around the world for more than twenty years. A home, JZ declares, is a spiritual realization and should reflect the passions of its owners.

Sophisticated French Country

RURAL WASHINGTON STATE

Approaching her home in rural Washington State with the same zest and feeling she has for her work, JZ has slowly remodeled a small, 1,100-square-foot, nondescript farmhouse adjoining her horse stables into a 20,000-square-foot mansion, combining the best of luxurious Scalamandré fabrics with elegant French antiques and charming "shabby chic" accessories to create a romantic retreat for herself and her constant stream of international guests and celebrities.

Her home, JZ emphasizes, is meant to be comfortable, a place where people can feel free to walk barefoot, sit down with a cup of coffee, and put up their feet. JZ designed it all herself, starting with her kitchen and slowly adding rooms as she could afford to do so. The house remains a work in progress: currently she is replacing contemporary fireplaces with hand-cut stone hearths and custom-designed mantels by Rose Tarlow. JZ has been assisted in the process by Nancy Trent, who has helped her find and acquire the choice fabrics and treasures. JZ emphasizes that a home is a reflection of oneself, and this is readily apparent as one feels the warmth and love this charismatic woman has given to every room's décor. 🌿

The breakfast room overlooking the pool has colorful draperies in Scalamandré "Caprice des Dames," a hand-printed rose-and-cream check on silk. A needlepoint area rug rests beneath the hand-painted table and chairs.

ABOVE *Scalamandré "Sunrise Plaid" warms up the kitchen, accented by colorful beaded lamp fringe.*

RIGHT *Miss Took, JZ's English bulldog, rests on a wicker chaise under a shady tree in the garden. Scalamandré's Island Cloth Collection "Polka Dot" in sky blue is used on the chaises.*

ABOVE *Thick, cut fringe lines a second set of portieres of sky blue "Colombine" silk damask on an adjacent archway. Powder blue "Adelaide" silk taffeta was used to line the damask for a soft accent. A second set of colorful, striped silk portieres is glimpsed behind the blue taffeta. The walnut commode is Louis XV.*

FACING *Anchored by an antique Savonnerie carpet, the dramatic two-story entrance foyer is flanked by a sweeping staircase carpeted in Aubusson panels that JZ found at the Paris flea market on one of her frequent shopping trips. The wrought-iron railings were handcrafted by a local artisan. A skirted center table is covered with Scalamandré "Meissen," an anis-colored lampas that features polychromatic flowering vines inspired by eighteenth-century Bavarian porcelain. An antique French crystal chandelier glows overhead.*

LEFT *Luxurious silk draperies cover every door, puddling softly on the floor. The archway at the back of the foyer is hung with Scalamandré's silk damask "Colombine" in a pale sky blue. A colorful pillow in "Calaban" cut velvet, accented by tassel fringe, rests on the Louis XV bergere.*

FACING *The formal living room rises eighteen feet and is framed by elegant draperies in "Provence" silk taffeta in pale blue and peach, with a swagged valance in pink and aqua "Clair de Lune." The sofa is upholstered in "Marquise" silk lampas in eggshell, and the chair in the foreground is covered with "Chick Austin Striped Floral," a documentary striped floral lampas reproduced for the Chick Austin House in Hartford, Connecticut. The ebonized coffee table was custom made by Rose Tarlow.*

FACING *Magnificent door drapery highlights the leaded-glass doors that lead into the living room. Constructed of elaborately draped and swagged, hand-printed faille "Clair de Lune" in pink and aqua, the drapery puddles opulently onto the floor.*

ABOVE *An antique rock crystal French wall sconce sparkles on the mirrored wall, with "Provence" silk taffeta window drapes reflected in the background.*

LEFT *Scalamandré's heavy, silk "Double-Banded" tassel fringe is used to highlight the "Clair de Lune" panels, which are held back with silk "Beehive" tassel tiebacks in a custom colorway.*

PREVIOUS OVERLEAF *The viewing room is intimate, arranged for playing chess and watching TV. A private garden centered on an antique European stone fountain was added to bring the outdoors inside. Comfortable furnishings are accented with Scalamandré "Nashville" silk damask embroidered pillow fronts on the sofa. An antique monk's bench was made into a coffee table.*

LEFT *A close view of the "Nashville" pillow fronts shows their intricate hand embroidery. Note the metallic gold thread. A looped fringe edges the pillows.*

FACING *A skirted table in the viewing room is covered with Scalamandré's silk liseré "Bee" in cream and gold, and a c. 1800 Meissen Chinaman lamp is in the background. Crystal boxes of truffles are quite popular with JZ's guests.*

LEFT   *A dramatic Lalique glass table in the dining room is surrounded by Rose Tarlow chairs covered in "Strawberry" silk liseré. Walls are upholstered in lampas "Melograno" in antique white. Melograno means pomegranate in Italian and has signified wealth and prosperity since ancient times. A c. 1810 Chinese export bowl rests in the center of the table.*

ABOVE   *Rose Tarlow ebonized and hand painted dining chairs are covered in Scalamandré "Strawberry" silk with bronze, turquoise, and gold tassel fringe. A pillow in "Titian" striped silk in aqua and silver is a comfortable accent.*

DAVID PARKER AND MIMI FINDLAY

David Parker, an architect as well as an interior designer, specializes in historic planning and design for both private and museum clients and has worked with Scalamandré on projects ranging from The Hermitage, President Andrew Jackson's home, to the U.S. Treasury's presidential reception rooms. Mimi Findlay, an interiors historian and preservationist, has guided the restoration and furnishing of nineteenth-century interiors, both public and private, in New Jersey, Connecticut, and New York.

An Aesthetic Movement Parlor

MANHATTAN

The owners of this six-story brownstone on New York City's Upper East Side had already worked with Parker and Findlay on their previous Manhattan residence; so, after purchasing the brownstone in 1998, they asked both designers to assist in its restoration. Built in 1882 on land acquired from Charles Tiffany, the brownstone had remained a single-family residence until 1976, when it was donated to a school and used as offices. In danger of being torn down for a high-rise, the building was rescued by the current owners, both of whom are passionate preservationists. While the majority of rooms still retained much of their ornate 1880s woodwork and detailing, the most important public space—the parlor—had been stripped of its rich, carved moldings and opulent wall coverings in 1925 and redecorated in the then-fashionable palette of white and gold.

The parlor of this Upper East Side 1882 brownstone has been returned to its original nineteenth-century elegance through diligent research and detective work. Fragments of the former wall covering were found between floor joists. The original taupe-and-gold-colored wallpaper had been designed to simulate a fancy jacquard, and Scalamandré re-created this custom design as a silk-and-linen brocatelle.

All of the woodwork was restored using shadows of the original pilasters and molding profiles on the walls. Aesthetic movement furnishings include an

upholstered suite of Herter Brothers furniture and a confidente with its original c. 1870 upholstery re-created by Scalamandré. The carpet is English needlepoint, c. 1860. The elaborate ceiling is a printed-and-gold-leaf treatment made to resemble mosaics, inspired by a Herter Brothers ceiling in the 1882 Governor Oliver Ames Mansion drawing room in Boston. Scalamandré also re-created the room's original hand-blocked, flocked frieze at the top of the walls on an embossed gold faille paper.

ABOVE *A detail of the rich color and design of the curtains, which are constructed of alternating bands of Scalamandré "Mercante di Venezia Rigatto" and the custom-woven multi-on-black silk lampas "Berry and Vine," are attributed to a Bruce Talbert design.*

FACING *The silk lampas found on the confidente, attributed to Bruce Talbert and re-created by Scalamandré as "Berry and Vine," was used with alternating bands of Scalamandré's cotton striped damask "Mercante di Venezia Rigatto" for the tall, swagged window curtains. A Herter Brothers rotating, rosewood easel holds an oil painting by J. G. Brown.*

FACING *An inlaid and carved Aesthetic movement confidente was found for the center of the parlor, and during its restoration a fragment of the original silk was uncovered under one arm. Believed to have been designed by the well-known English Aesthetic movement designer Bruce Talbert, the fabric was reproduced by Scalamandré in a custom multi-on-black silk lampas named "Berry and Vine."*

LEFT *A fragment of the original silk lampas found on the confidente during restoration rests on Scalamandré's beautiful and exacting re-creation. Underneath the fragment remnant lies a copy of the book published by Bruce Talbert in Boston in 1878 containing his drawings and elevations, which were used as inspiration for the parlor during its extensive renovation.*

BELOW *Portieres between the parlor and dining room are also designed with alternating bands of Scalamandré's damask "Mercante di Venezia Rigatto" and the custom-woven "Berry and Vine" silk lampas. Scalamandré re-created the gold silk-and-linen brocatelle on the walls from original wallpaper that simulated a taupe-and-gold fancy jacquard that was found beneath the floor boards.*

Scalamandré Homes 159

Richard and Linda Delier have run a successful design business, the Interior Shop in Buck's County, Pennsylvania, for more than ten years. Several years ago they decided to build a new home for their retirement, since, although their children had left, their family was still large, when you count their five Yorkies and one cat. Richard had found house plans for a home in a magazine in 1980 that was unique in that it had no formal living or dining room, just a forty-foot-long great room across the back of the house, with a farm kitchen at one end and a twenty-foot stone fireplace at the other: Perfect, the Deliers both decided, for the relaxed lifestyle they wanted for their retirement.

Elegant Country Retirement

PENNSYLVANIA

Located in bucolic Buck's County, Pennsylvania, the property has pasture fences and a picturesque stone bridge over a dry creek bed. The abundant wildlife—including quails, pheasants, turkeys, fox, deer, red-tail hawks and mice—guided the Deliers' design decisions. Scalamandré "Edwin's Covey," a hand-printed union cloth featuring quails and flowers, was the natural choice for the great room drapery. The quails in the fabric were copied as the logo for the property's sign, and even incorporated into a custom carpet for the great room, which was woven with a quail in each corner.

A French lit-style mahogany sofa flanking the stone fireplace was upholstered in "Highland Fling," Scalamandré's hand-printed paisley velvet in rich reds and sage, and a Louis XV–style wing chair was updated in the rich reds, browns, and greens of "Venetian Stripe" to complement the paisley sofa. More quail were found for the foyer and staircase with "L'Olseau," a brown Scalamandré toile wallpaper that was a perfect color match for the carpeting.

The great room in the Deliers' country home stretches forty feet across the entire back of the house and is anchored on one end by a massive stone fireplace. French doors open out to a bucolic view and the pool. The windows are framed with the cheery mustard yellow of "Edwin's Covey," a hand-printed union cloth, with trim in "Edwin's Tassel Fringe" scalloped silk tassel fringe. A French lit-style sofa is upholstered in Scalamandré's colorful paisley "Highland Fling" and piled high with cushions. The wildlife theme was carried through to the carpet, which was custom woven with quail in the corners, repeating those in the "Edwin's Covey" drapes.

The master suite, off the great room, was designed in a whimsical theme using "Ming Circus" as the drapery fabric, a hand-printed cotton chintz featuring a contented panda munching bamboo, along with storks, baboons and acrobats. The Yorkies have their own four-poster bed in the master suite, trimmed, of course, in Scalamandré fabrics including "Dauphine," "Mayfair Plaid," "Powers Court" and "Kate," complete with silk tassels and fringe. "Pillement Toile" in a cool slate was used for drapery and wallpaper in the adjoining master bath for a sophisticated look.

Upstairs, the Jack and Jill bathroom shared by two guest rooms was done in silk "Jour de Juin" and its companion wallpaper, which feature a theme of bugs—quite popular with the grandchildren. And, of course, the guest bedroom drapery fabric has Buck's County bugs—and even mice—in it with Scalamandré "Stravagante," a hand-printed cotton percale. Casually elegant and yet livable, the Deliers' home shows that you can enjoy beautiful fabrics and furnishings in a home with five dogs and a cat!

ABOVE *A Louis XV–style armchair has been updated with "Venetian Stripe," a Scalamandré documentary carpet in warm reds, greens and browns. The hand-embroidered pillow features a Yorkie, naturally.*

RIGHT *The Deliers and their dogs have their own four-poster beds in the master suite. A whimsical theme was chosen for the curtains and table skirt using "Ming Circus," a hand-printed cotton chintz featuring acrobats swinging amongst a happy baboon, an aristocratic stork and a panda. "Edward's" scalloped silk tassel fringe was used for the trim in camel, fern, wine and peacock. French doors open onto the patio and softly rolling meadows beyond.*

The Yorkies have their own four-poster bed upholstered in the finest Scalamandre fabrics. The quilt and face are made from "Dauphine," a striped lampas in blues on yellow strie, while the bed pillows, dust ruffle, and curtain lining were constructed in Scalamandré's "Mayfair Plaid," a crisp yellow-and-blue plaid taffeta. Bed pillows were done in "Powers Court," a blue strie silk taffeta and "Kate," a blue liseré with strawberries.

FACING, LEFT *A detail of the master bath drapes in slate-colored "Pillement Toile" edged in a small-check ruffle.*

LEFT *"Pillement Toile" wallpaper with matching linen drapes sets a sophisticated tone for the master bath. The cool slate color of the wallpaper accentuates the gold and silver fittings in the room.*

ABOVE *The guest bedroom, done in soft buttercup yellow, is accented with drapery in Scalamandré "Stravagante," a hand-printed cotton percale. The design is based on paintings by the famous seventeenth-century painter Giovanna Garzoni, considered the finest botanical artist of the seventeenth century. Her works were commissioned by the Medici family.*

ABOVE *Frogs, crickets and spiders crawl across the "Jour de Juin" silk bath stool, which is edged with Scalamandré "Brompton Plaid" cotton in limerick on ivory and accented by "Scallop" loop fringe in lime.*

FACING *Bugs abound in the Jack and Jill guest bath, with "Jour de Juin" wallpaper in pastels on white, with matching "Jour de Juin" silk drapes. Notice that even the drawer pulls are bugs. The "Jour de Juin" pattern of insects and reptiles was inspired by an eighteenth-century embroidered waistcoat.*

Pillows in "Calabassas County" outdoor printed Island Cloth Collection enliven the pool with bright green frogs leaping across a hot-pink background. The chaise is covered in Island Cloth Collection "Guadeloupe" in a sunny sunflower yellow.

Country Retreat

WESTCHESTER COUNTY, NEW YORK

Robert Bitter, co-president of Scalamandre, always enjoys a design challenge. So, when he was offered the opportunity to rescue a derelict cottage in Westchester County, he readily agreed. Over a period of five months, Bob enlisted the help of East Hampton designer Peter Faulk and a local contractor, Scott Henriques, to transform the rundown 1920s cottage into a cozy retreat for himself and his friends.

Bob especially loved the location of the property, nestled on the edge of the piney Woods Preserve. Set back twenty-five yards from the road, the small, limestone-colored structure was surrounded by three acres of lawns. Every evening Canadian geese would fly over the gables and stone chimneys of the house and land on the narrow ponds below. It was a simple and welcome oasis away from the hectic pace of New York City.

The most appealing aspect of the interior was the arched stone fireplace. It reminded Bob of his Aunt Patricia's Pocono mountain farm. And, more importantly, the fireplace would keep the entire cottage warm and comfortable. during the notoriously severe northern Westchester winters.

Using the fireplace's rugged character as the starting point, Bob and Peter created a masculine retreat with a soft edge. "Edwin's Covey," a Scalamandre printed linen blend whose design was inspired by Bob's father Edwin's love of hunting was used to cover the four windows of the living room, a small upholstered club chair and several sofa pillows. "Highland Fling," a hand-printed, brushed-cotton paisley velvet in rusty red, green and gold was chosen to slipcover a mid-eighteenth-century Philadelphia wing chair for an elegant yet rustic look. Turkish prayer carpets were made into large, comfortable floor pillows and backed with "Venetian Stripe" ingrain, and the room was anchored by a classic, hand-knotted Oriental carpet.

A small alcove off the living room was made into an inviting dining space. "Edwin's Covey" was carried through as the window treatment and accented with woolen "Balmoral Plaid" seat covers in rusty reds, greens and golds. A heavily distressed walnut gateleg table became the focal point of the space, adding a note of old-world charm.

Bob used a combination of family pieces, such as his grandfather's nineteenth-century sled, along with Audubon prints, vintage earthenware and weaving paraphernalia from the Scalamandre mill to create a cozy, comfortable and personal retreat. ❧

Robert Bitter, co-president of Scalamandré, relaxes in the living room of his rustic retreat in upstate New York. The room is centered on a stone fireplace that heats the home nicely during the winter. It is furnished in Scalamandré fabrics inspired by the countryside. "Edwin's Covey" in a soft, creamy sisal color, accented by multicolored silk tassel fringe, was used for drapery treatments and for upholstering an overstuffed chair. "Highland Fling," a hand-printed paisley cotton velvet in sage and red slipcovers the comfortable Philadelphia wing chair—Bob's favorite spot for reading.

ABOVE *The kitchen is enlivened with a scarlet Roman shade of "Bon Oeuf," a hand-printed cotton percale featuring eggs. A valance in "Gallo Macchia," a hand-printed cotton percale in Florentine gold, sports cocky roosters.*

FACING *The dining room chairs are covered with "Balmoral," a 100 percent worsted wool in old gold and olive on brick for a warm and colorful accent. More color is added with "Venetian Stripes," a vertical-striped carpet in traditional ingrain width (36 inches). Curtains in "Edwin's Covey" help coordinate the dining and living rooms, which flow into each other.*

MELINDA SULLIVAN AND ROBERT KEVIN CASSIDY

Melinda Sullivan has had a passion for passementerie as long as she can remember. She fondly recalls, as a little girl, proudly holding herself very still so her mother could tie the bow on the back of her dress just right. Her love of bows and trimmings has continued as an adult, and when she and her husband, Paul, bought their 1929 West Hartford Colonial Revival in 1993, it became the perfect showplace for her passion.

Colonial Revival

HARTFORD, CONNECTICUT

The twenty-room stone home set on four acres was built in classic Colonial Revival style, and fortunately had never been significantly altered. With the assistance of designer Robert Kevin Cassidy, Melinda set about upgrading the interior, adding the conveniences of the twenty-first century while retaining the ambience and elegance of the 1930s. Thus, details such as warm butternut paneling and the sweeping, curved staircase in the large foyer were retained, while a dramatic two-story kitchen fitted with the most modern appliances and accessories replaced a warren of small rooms in the redbrick servants' wing. French doors and a terrace were added to the back of the large living room, opening it to views of the back gardens, while details such as intricate cornices and moldings were left intact.

The living room walls were painted in apricot and then given a ruby glaze, resulting in a pale salmon color that is warm and welcoming. Elaborate draperies were designed with Scalamandré's warp-printed silk "Versailles," accented by four-inch, custom mold fringe and "Marie Antoinette" rosette double tiebacks. Drapery cornices in an elaborate chinoiserie pattern were designed by Cassidy using details from a Chippendale mirror hung between the windows. Passementerie was added throughout the rest of the home: each bed is draped with beautiful fabrics and trims, and even the master bath has Scalamandré custom mold fringe in an elaborate, alternating-flame-and-spiral design. As Melinda points out, passementerie adds another dimension and texture, the finishing touch that makes a textile special. ✄

The living room, which extends across the width of the house, is painted in a warm, pale salmon. Elaborate draperies with gilded chinoiserie-style cornices were designed for the windows with Scalamandré "Versailles," a warp-printed silk.

The Chippendale mirror between the draperies provided the inspiration for the design of the cornices. Furniture in the room is a blend of fine English and American antiques.

LEFT *Elaborate, gilded cornices crown the top of the window draperies. Scalamandré's warp-printed silk "Versailles" is accented by custom mold fringe*

FACING *Hand-painted silver wallpaper in an Oriental theme adds an elegant note to the master bath. Striped silk draperies are accented with a custom Scalamandré four-inch mold fringe.*

FACING   *An antique four-poster canopied bed in a guest bedroom is dressed with swagged valances accented by silk tassel fringe.*

ABOVE   *Scalamandré's silk tassel fringe in tobacco, cream, pomegranate and teal highlight the swagged valance of a four-poster bed.*

RIGHT   *Scalamandré's handmade, custom-wrapped mold fringe in pale gold, green and ivory features alternating silk bands in flame and spiral designs.*

Prestwould
Southern Neoclassic

MECKLENBURG COUNTY, VIRGINIA

Prestwould is one of the most complete surviving plantations in the South. Built between 1794 and 1795 by Sir Peyton Skipworth for his second wife, Lady Jean Skipworth, in Mecklenburg County, Virginia, near the Roanoke River, the plantation was originally furnished by Lady Skipworth with exquisite eighteenth-century English botanical wallpapers, fine English and American furniture, and the largest library assembled by a woman in eighteenth-century America.

Following Lady Skipworth's death in 1826, Prestwould was redecorated in the Neoclassical style by her daughter-in-law, Lelia Robertson Skipworth. French scenic wallpaper with deep Neoclassical borders and panel papers were installed, along with Baltimore painted furniture and high-style Empire furnishings. The plantation remained in the family until 1914, when it was sold and its contents dispersed at auction.

When Prestwould was acquired by the Roanoke River Museum in 1963, it was discovered that, fortunately, over 10,000 original documents relating to the house and its furnishings had survived. Work began in earnest on conservation and restoration, and today the plantation has recovered nearly 80 percent of its original furnishings, making it one of the most complete existing examples of ante-bellum plantation life from the 1790s to the 1840s. Prestwould is notable for the survival of many of its historic wallpapers, with unusually complete documentation of their purchase and installation. Fragments found during restoration were combined with

Sir Peyton's Chamber has been restored to its c. 1805 appearance using the original inventory. Scalamandré reproduced the colorful "Leaf and Sprig" English wallpaper along with the "Narrow Oak Leaf Border," the scraps of which were found behind plumbing in a closet during a 1989 restoration. A tent bed with mahogany cornice by Samuel White (1796) is dressed in Scalamandré's reproduction of the 1790s brick-red-on-ecru toile "Fern and Thistle," as is an eastern Virginia easy chair, c. 1790.

Photographs courtesy of Prestwould.

ABOVE *Prestwould, a seven-bay, hip-roofed Georgian plantation built in Virginia between 1794 and 1795, was constructed of sand limestone quarried on the plantation. Built for Sir Peyton Skipworth and his second wife, Lady Jean Skipworth, it was one of the largest eighteenth-century houses built in Virginia and is now considered one of the most intact early plantation houses surviving in the South.*

FACING *The parlor has been returned to its 1790s appearance, hung with Scalamandré's reproduction of Lady Skipworth's 1790s English paper "Angle Leaf," with its accompanying "Reed and Ribbon Border." A portrait of Sarah Nivison Skipworth hangs on the wall.*

Lady Skipworth's papers to re-create and reinstall the wallpapers. Scalamandré produced several of these important documentary papers for Prestwould, including "Angle Leaf" and its accompanying "Reed and Ribbon Border" used in the parlor, the delicate "Leaf and Sprig" with "Narrow Oak Leaf Border" used in Sir Peyton's Chamber (c. 1805) (scraps of which were found behind plumbing in a closet during restoration) and "White Satin Grass" with "Laurel Leaf Border," the most expensive of the papers used in the drawing room (fragments of which were found behind two large pier glasses). ❧

A Postmodern Villa

Salvador Dali, Pablo Picasso, Alexander Calder, Joan Miro—are all important names of modern art that we take for granted today. But much of the popularity of modern art in the United States is credited to Chick Austin, the colorful and provocative director of Hartford's Wadsworth Athenaeum, who, in 1927 at the age of twenty-six, began introducing modern art to this conservative insurance capital, thus beginning a revolution in art between the world wars. Austin mounted the first major retrospective on Picasso in this country, staged shocking operas and plays by Gertrude Stein and Virgil Thomson at the Athenaeum, and embraced all of the modern art forms in his museum, from photography to contemporary music.

During his honeymoon in Italy in the summer of 1929, Austin discovered the Palladian-style, sixteenth-century Villa Ferretti in the town of Dolo, and after returning to Hartford used it as a model to build a villa of his own. Set back from the staid Colonial Revivals on two acres of land on a tree-lined Hartford residential street, the villa was built like a stage set—only eighteen feet deep but eighty-six feet long, thus presenting an imposing front façade. Austin's villa is considered by many to be one of the first examples of postmodern architecture in the country. Austin furnished his home in an eclectic style, combining fine European antiques with Modern movement art in a stimulating manner. Luminaries such as George Balanchine, Salvador Dali, Gertrude Stein, and others were frequent visitors to the home.

The sunken living room has been restored to its 1930s splendor using vintage photographs taken for a December 1930 article in the Hartford Courant *and original paint samples and carpet fragments. Walls were returned to their original color, a dark blue-green meant to match the sky in the large, c. 1730 Italian tempera panels that were hung throughout the room. Painted rope work borders on the panels in two shades of rose were copied for the colors of the carpet—which Scalamandré reproduced as a Wilton cut pile in rose—and the misty rose silk curtains. Scalamandré produced a luscious silk jacquard called "Chick Austin Striped Floral Lampas" for the Venetian sofa and bergeres. An art deco green leather coffee table, c. 1945, provides a modern accent.*

The family donated the house to Wadsworth Athenaeum in 1985, and it was designated a National Historic Landmark. Restoration has continued on the house over the past twenty years, returning it to the décor of the 1930s. Scalamandré has been involved with many aspects of the restoration, from supplying fabrics for the English and Venetian antique furniture to re-creating the brocatelle hung on the dining room walls based on period images and fragments found in the house. Work continues: currently Scalamandré is reproducing a French toile for the hallway.

ABOVE   *The front façade of the Chick Austin House is patterned after an Italian villa. Only eighteen feet deep, it was designed to produce a grand impression and has been called the first postmodern building in this country when it was constructed in 1930.*

FACING   *"Julius," a cotton-and-silk blue strie satin was used to re-cover the c. 1810 English settee; the fabric's color is a perfect match for the dusky blue in the tempera wall panels.*

Photographs courtesy of Prestwould.

ABOVE *"Classic Point," a silk damask, was custom dyed in a French blue for the Louis XV armchairs.*

FACING *A pair of painted Venetian bergeres—nineteenth-century replicas of eighteenth-century furniture—was restored with "Chick Austin Striped Floral Lampas" in beige with blue stripes. The colors were based on the Austins' son David's recollections of the room in combination with black-and-white period photographs.*

ABOVE *The delicate rococo lines of the c. 1740 gild-ed-and-painted Sicilian commode are reflected in the patterns of the "Chick Austin Brocatelle" used to uphol-ster the walls.*

FACING *Chick Austin found a c.1730 German rococo bed niche on his European honeymoon in 1929 and had it built in as the focal point of the dining room. The walls were covered in a striking blue-green, silk-and-*

linen, distressed, complex jacquard, "Chick Austin Brocatelle," which Scalamandré reproduced from period photographs and remnants, even matching the seams and repeats exactly. The walls, curtains and valances have now been restored to their original splendor with the brocatelle. The Louis XVI–style dining table is the room's original and is set with the family's silver. The Louis XV chairs are upholstered in "Chick Austin Twill," a custom peacock blue silk.

FACING *A French toile of a chinoiserie scene found in the hallway is being painstakingly reproduced by Scalamandré in France. Pictured here is a faded original panel, on the left, next to a recent fabric strike-off.*

ABOVE *Chick Austin loved to sew and constructed the original dining room draperies himself. Shown here are his sewing machine and an original fragment of the silk brocatelle that Scalamandré reproduced.*

Villa Louis

WESTERN WISCONSIN

In 1885, Hercules Louis Dousman and his wife, Nina Sturgis Dousman, began an extensive redecoration of their country home, Villa Louis, in Prairie du Chien in western Wisconsin. The grand Italianate home, built along the banks of the Mississippi River, was the center of a sprawling estate. The Chicago decorating firm hired by the Dousmans sent an expatriate Englishman, Joseph Twyman, to supervise the project. Twyman was a strong William Morris devotee, having met him in England; he used a number of Morris wallpapers and fabrics in the Dousman home.

By 1886, Villa Louis had been handsomely redecorated in the newly fashionable Arts and Crafts style and remained Prairie du Chien's most distinguished private home through the late nineteenth and into the early twentieth century. But as family members died or moved away, Villa Louis slowly declined in status, until by 1913 the last family moved out and the home was leased first to a boys' school and then to owners of a boarding house. In 1934, the

Villa Louis front hall 1895 and 2003. Redecorated in the newly fashionable English Arts and Crafts style in 1886, the front hall presented visitors with a comfortable and welcoming appearance. Restoration has returned the hall to its 1890s elegance, with a block-printed reproduction of the Arts and Crafts–style wallpaper, along with Scalamandré's reproduction of William Morris's 1876 "Acanthus," a cotton velvet in deep red and pink on an off-white ground, which was used for two sets of portieres and furniture upholstery. Much of the original furnishings, from the overhead chandelier to a blackamoor card receiver, have, fortunately, survived.

Photographs courtesy of Villa Louis.

surviving family decided to donate their home to the city as a museum, in an effort to help preserve their history. To prepare the house for opening to the public, many of the remaining Arts and Crafts details were removed and placed in storage. Initially described as an "antebellum mansion," Villa Louis became a popular tourist attraction. It wasn't until 1995 that restoration of the house was undertaken to return it to its Arts and Crafts origins of the 1890s.

Scalamandré has been instrumental, reproducing many of the original Morris patterns with such a degree of accuracy that two were recently chosen for use at Kelmscott Manor, Morris's country estate in England. Scalamandré has reproduced "Acanthus," a cotton velvet in deep red and pink on an off-white ground; , which was used on several chairs, a sofa, an ottoman and two sets of portieres in the main hall. "Windrush," a surface-printed cotton in blues with light and dark brown and white accents, was reproduced from two surviving curtain panels for the dining room. "Marigold," was reproduced for curtain and portiere panels in the

The dining room in 1890 was redecorated with lavish bronze-gold wallpaper and a dado of mahogany-glazed Lincrusta Walton. Scalamandré reproduced "Windrush"— a Morris pattern registered in October 1883—from the original surviving textiles as a printed cotton in cream, blues and brown and used it in the curtain panels. The original sideboard and china cabinet remain in place, where they display a fine collection of silver, glass and ceramics all original to the house.

master bedroom and dressing room; it is a bright madder-red-on-crème-ground printed cotton. "The Royal Burgundy," a design by Thomas Wardle (who worked for Morris), was reproduced by Scalamandré for the parlor using faded panels to extract details. And another Wardle design whose name was not known was reproduced as "Villa Louis Persian Thistle." A printed cotton velvet in dark and light blues on a crème ground, "Persian Thistle" was used for portiere panels in the opening of the parlor bay window.

While restoration continues on several bedrooms, Villa Louis has now been returned to its former status as an exemplary Arts and Crafts beauty of the late nineteenth century. ✺

The southwest corner of the parlor is centered on a generous bay window that still holds its original marble statue of Violet and Virginia, the Dousmans' oldest daughters. Scalamandré has reproduced a Thomas Wardle 1884 cotton velvet, "Villa Louis Persian Thistle," which was used for two portiere panels dressing the opening of the bay window. The reproduction was so exacting that Kelmscott Manor, William Morris's country home in England, has chosen this textile for its own restoration. Scalamandré also reproduced Wardle's 1882 "The Royal Burgundy," another printed cotton velvet, for two of the parlor windows.

The Details

Details are what make the difference, and nowhere is this more apparent than in textiles and upholstery. Here are some of our favorite trimmings and fabrics to help give an idea of the rich world of possibilities that awaits with Scalamandré.

FACING   *"Tulip" fringe and braid in wedgwood, gold and cherry
are as delicate as miniature, handmade flowers.*

ABOVE   *"Edward's Collection" extravagant, silk fringe in old gold,
fern and wine is popular for trimming ottomans and chairs.*

ABOVE   *"Hampton Court" mold fringe in red, beige and lime is one of Scalamandré's more exuberant fringes, inspired by the lush, fragrant gardens of Hampton Court Castle in England.*

FACING   *"Le Mans," a hand-woven, open-scroll braid is available in a dozen colorways, including fern and coral as pictured here.*

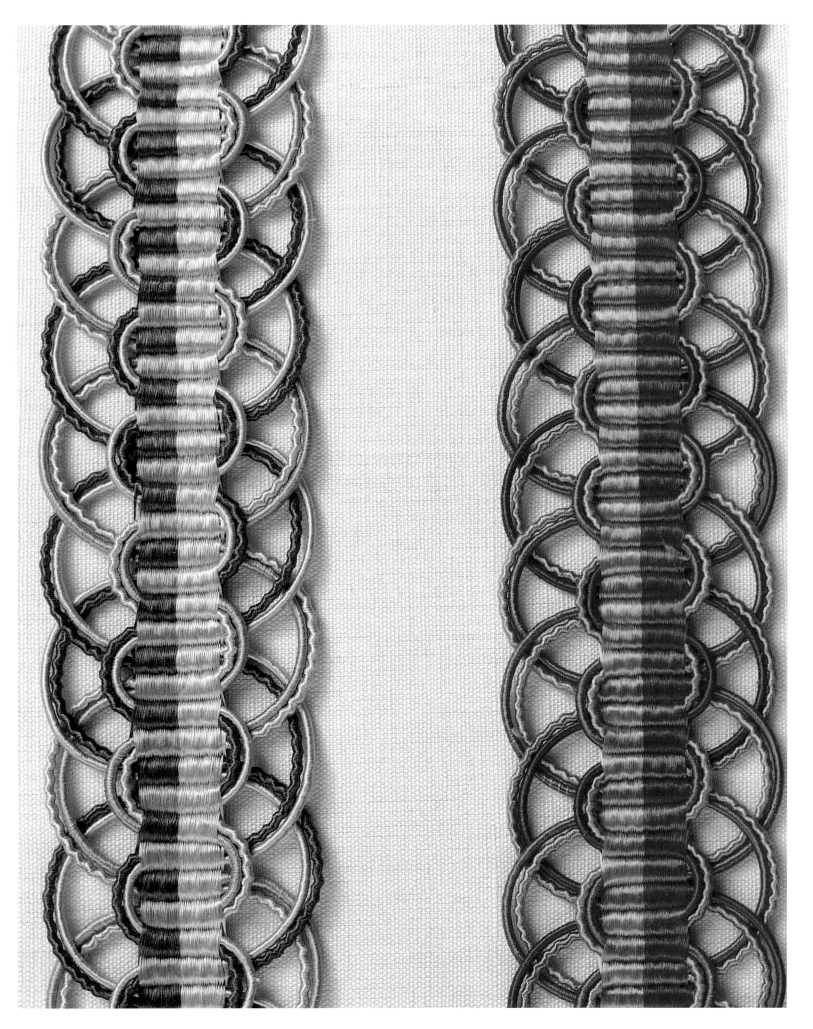

FACING *"Oiseau des Exotique," a silk, warp-printed taffeta is one of Scalamandré's most sophisticated and complicated textiles. A lengthy and delicate process of loose weaving, printing, unpicking and re-weaving at two mills—one for weaving and one for printing—is required. The result is exquisite.*

ABOVE *"Gran Conde," a silk cut and uncut velvet nestles underneath the corresponding gold silk tassel trim and tieback.*

Scalamandré's Boudoir Chair is upholstered in "La Perouse" lampas in white on antique gold, with complementary bullion fringe trim. The throw pillow in "Monroe Bee" correlates with the insect motif of the chair fabric. Curtains in "Shimmer Silk" with thick "Hampton Court" mold fringe and tieback frame the exotic and colorful "Shanghai" wallpaper behind.

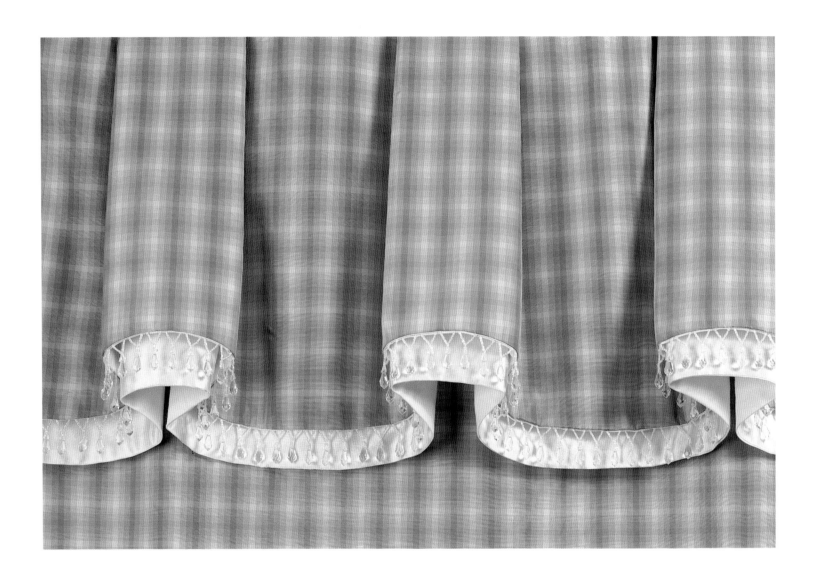

ABOVE *"Domenico Plaid" in a cheerful green-and-ivory silk is made into curtains finished with crystal fringe.*

FACING *"Jacobean," a chenille tapestry in multicolor on maize, evokes the beauty of Old England.*

FACING "Duncan," in wool, cotton and spun rayon, is a colorful
Gothic Revival–inspired epinglé in multi navy and maize on
crimson. Epinglé is a French term used to describe a fine, looped
pile created by warp yarns that float over a weft-inserted rod or pin.
Once the loop is created, the rod or pin is removed. "Duncan" has
both looped and cut portions of the worsted wool–faced design.

ABOVE "Blue Mythology," a printed cotton toile, is highlighted by
scenes of French maidens and cherubs.

TR18039

FX4201

V9474

FX4072A

T2752

T2862

T2929

FX4 I2

ST18053

FACING *Passementerie is often compared to the confection on a cake. Here some of the best of Scalamandré's trims and tassels are displayed, quite appropriately and cleverly, as cakes.*

ABOVE *"Duchessa" trims and tiebacks incorporate whimsical jade accents, including a silk double tieback in red, green and gold with a Chinese yellow-jade medallion, silk trim featuring* a yellow-jade chicken and mold tassels, a key tassel with a jade turtle, and a rosette in red, green and gold sporting a jade turtle. The "Duchessa" trim is displayed against "Nashville" silk damask in cardinal. "Nashville" was reproduced for The Hermitage in Nashville, Tennessee. Based on c. 1830 Chinese export material, "Nashville" was used for parlor curtains

FACING   *The rich colors of "Muriel" trims in jewel include silk tassel fringe, a silk rosette with mold hangers, a smaller rosette with tassel, and a colorful silk key tassel. The "Muriel" trim is highlighted against cardinal "Nashville" silk damask.*

ABOVE   *A gold-on-federal-blue silk lampas with the presidential seal was designed by Scalamandré for the Blue Room of the White House for Jackie Kennedy in the early 1960s. A double-tassel tieback in federal blue and gold was part of the commission.*

FACING   *One of Scalamandré's most complex mold tassels, this Greek Revival work of art was painstakingly reproduced for the historic Old Merchant's House museum in New York City. This intricate tassel is eleven inches long and took weeks to make by hand. The backdrop fabric is the "Kykuit Dining Room" brocatelle, recently reproduced for the Rockefeller estate in Tarrytown, New York.*

ABOVE   *"Venetian Carnival," a hand-printed cotton chintz, is inspired by the Italian grotesques of the sixteenth and seventeenth centuries, which combined mythological and allegorical elements with arabesque patterns and design.*

ABOVE *"Neptune's Treasure," a hand-printed cotton in red and taupe on gold, was inspired by a small room in the Pitti Palace in Florence, whose ceiling is decorated entirely in delicately painted shells. Note the intricate seaweed accents.*

FACING *"Stravagante," a hand-painted cotton percale, features fruits, flowers, bugs and even a pair of tiny mice. The design was inspired by the famous paintings of Giovanna Garzoni (1600–1670), who was considered the finest botanical painter of the seventeenth century and who enjoyed the patronage of the Medici family.*

ABOVE *"Cherub Print," a hand-printed union cloth in new colors of pinks and yellow on celadon, was first designed by Adriana Bitter in 1947, when she was a teenager, for the restoration of William Randolf Hearst's San Simeon Castle in California, based on architectural motifs in the main reception room. It can still be seen at Hearst's Castle today.*

RIGHT *"Parfait," a contemporary jacquard in corals and celadon, creates a ribbon latticework effect.*

ABOVE *Cupid offers a toast in "Cupido," Scalamandré's hand-printed cotton toile on a yellow ground, a reproduction of an early-nineteenth-century toile de Jouy.*

RIGHT *The White House of the Confederacy in Richmond, Virginia, commissioned Scalamandré to custom reproduce this massive, fourteen-inch double tieback in a documentary gold-on-brick silk for their restoration. The tieback rests on "Villa Louis" silk-and-linen brocatelle, a naturalistic Rococo Revival jacquard.*

A Glossary of Decorating Terms

Abaca A hard fiber from the leaf stems around the trunk of the abaca plant, *Musa textilis (Agotai),* which is of the same family as the banana and native to the Philippine Islands and Central America. Also called Manila hemp. Synonyms: Cebu hemp and Davao hemp. Also spelled Abaka. *See also* Hemp.

Abrasion resistance Acetate: Man-made fiber composed of acetylated cellulose.

Acid dyes Class of dyes used for protein & nylon fibers.

Acrylic Man-made fiber derived from petrochemical by-products.

Acrylic backing A treatment sometimes used for upholstery and direct application wall fabric. Wallcovering generally requires a heavier treatment.

Aniline An organic base for many dyestuffs and drugs derived from coal tar or petroleum chemicals. First distilled from indigo *(annil)* in 1826 by O. Unverdorben. Aniline's commercial importance stems from discovery of mauve by Sir William Henry Perkins in 1856.

Antique satin A satin weave cloth with an exaggerated slub weft and a fine warp.

Avora see Trevira

Axminster Popular cut-pile carpets woven on a complex loom invented in Yonkers, New York. They were popularized in Axminster, England, and were woven 27 to 36 inches wide in multicolor. They are available in wider widths today in a variety of fibers.

Balloon cloth A fine, densely set, plain-woven cloth of combed and carded long-staple cotton.

Bangtail A clipped weft float that forms a fringe.

Bar marks *(barré)* An irregularity in the appearance of fabric consisting of textural or color bars in the direction of the weft. Bar marks can be caused by irregularities in the yarn thickness, uneven dyeing, or the variation of pick density during the starting and stopping of the loom. *Barré* effects are sometimes intentionally created.

Barathea A twill variation with a broken rib weave on one face and a pebbly texture on the other.

Bark cloth Nonwoven material made from soaked and beaten inner bark of tropical trees. This term was also used during the fabulous fifties to describe a textured plain fabric, usually of cotton and linen blend.

Basket weave A variation of plain weave in which two or more warp ends and an equal number of weft picks are woven as one, creating a woven basket effect.

Batik A resist print in which wax is placed onto a fabric before dyeing in a specific design that will resist the color during the dyeing process.

Batiste A fine, sheer, plain-woven cloth of combed and carded cotton.

Batten On some types of hand looms, a batten can be a flat piece of wood shaped like a sword to beat the weft into place. On mechanical looms, a long, thin metal comb, held by a shifting frame, is used to align the weft, or filler yarn.

Beaker dyeing Dyeing of small samples, usually used for color approvals or specifications.

Beam A cylinder attached to the loom on which the warp is wound.

Bedford cloth A weave similar to piqué in which supplementary warp ends pad a vertically channeled fabric.

Bengaline A horizontal rib-effect, medium-weight textile originally used for apparel. It was named for Bengal, India, and was generally woven with silk yarns, sometimes in combination with cotton or wool.

Berber yarn A thick, hand-spun yarn of mottled natural wool.

Bird's-eye Traditional dobby weave diaper pattern of concentric diamonds. A large-scale bird's-eye is called a goose-eye.

Blanket A textile sample, showing a series of colors created by various warp and weft colors.

Bleaching A basic finishing process by which gray goods are scoured and whitened. Bleaching a fabric that has already been dyed is called stripping.

Bleeding A fault in which dyestuff runs from one pattern area into another. Usually not determined until the fabric becomes wet.

Block printing General term for a hand printing process using wood or linoleum blocks into which patterns have been cut.

Blooming Bulking yarns to create a fuller, softer cloth. Usually done with brushing.

Blotch Refers to the background area of a printed fabric or wallpaper.

Bobbinet A fine net with a six-sided knit mesh.

Bobbin lace A single-element construction, originally handmade on a pillow with numerous threads.

Boiling off A process of removing the sericin (gum) from raw silk yarn or raw silk fabric. Also, a scouring process for fabric coming off the loom that releases grease, gum, or sizing added to yarn during production.

Bolt An entire length of fabric, usually rolled full width on a tube, sometimes folded before rolling.

Boucle A novelty yarn that is looped and crimped to produce a pebbly surface.

Bourette An irregular, slubbed, spun yarn or fabric made from noil silk.

Bows Bows are made of multiple loops in the shape of a bow, and applied on swags, valances, and along with other trimmings.

Braid A corded gimp, open work or plaited narrow-width woven. Typically in widths of a half-inch to four inches, these trimmings are used to cover staples, glue and nails on upholstery, wall coverings and window treatments. Braids can also be a decorative accent.

Broadcloth   Originally the opposite of narrow cloth. Modern term refers to a host of qualities, but often thought of as an English twill weave; in worsted yarns, worsted which may be processed, such as felting.

Brocade   A very rich, multicolored jacquard cloth that is hand woven with many weft shuttles. It has an appearance of embroidery work, although the weft yarns used to create the multicolors are woven during the weaving process. These yarns float on the reverse side of the cloth only where the design appears. Less than one meter a day is woven.

Brocatelle   A two-dimensional high-relief jacquard cloth in which the main warp weaves a warp satin in the design area, and commonly a twill in the ground. A linen weft is used to raise the design areas to create an embossed appearance.

Broché   A wool, silk or man-made fiber fabric woven with a combination of plain and pile weave, the pile weave forming the pattern.

Broken twill   Twill weave with diagonal lines interrupted to create a stepped effect.

Buckram   A plain-woven cotton fabric stiffened with sizing.

Bullion   Bullion fringe has a high degree of twist, revealing a soft, rounded lower skirt edge. Bullion is typically used on the lower edges of furniture and on window treatments.

Burlap   A plain-woven cloth of round single-ply jute.

Burn-out fabric   A fabric or lace made with two different yarns with a pattern effect produced by destroying one of the yarns in a printing process that employs chemicals instead of color.

Calendering   A finishing process producing a flat, glossy, smooth surface by passing the fabric under pressure between a series of heated cylinders.

Calico   Originally cloth of linen and cotton from Calicut, India. Modern terminology refers to cottons often printed with small, simple designs.

Cannelé   A repp woven with two sets of warps; the first is a single yarn that acts as the foundation. The alternate warp end is plied to form a small rib in the vertical direction.

Cannetille   A lace or military braid made with gold or silver thread.

Canvas   A dense cloth, originally cotton, in twill or plain weave.

Carbonizing   A finishing process that destroys vegetable matter in wool cloth.

A third-floor winding machine transfers yarn from the skeins held on the swifts to the cones.

Carding   The process of straightening, untangling and cleaning fibers before spinning them into yarn.

Casement   A general term for sheer drapery fabric.

Cashmere   A fine fiber obtained from the undercoat of the Himalayan Cashmir goat.

Cavalry twill   A fancy, steep twill, originally worsted, which produces a tightly woven cloth.

Cellulose   Organic fibrous substance found in all vegetation that is the basic constituent of both natural and man-made cellulosic fibers such as cotton, linen, jute and rayon.

Chain stitch   An ornamental stitch resembling the links of a chain.

Challis   A sheer, plain-woven, lightly brushed fabric of wool, worsted or similarly textured man-made yarns. Originated in England in 1830.

Chambray   Smooth, lustrous, plain-weave cloth with yarn-dyed warp and white weft.

Cheesecloth   Soft, plain-woven, low-count, inexpensive cotton. Sometimes called gauze.

Chenille   Derived from the French for "caterpillar." A special yarn with pile protruding on all sides.

Chevron   A herringbone weave in a zigzag, diagonal pattern.

Chiffon   Plain-weave, soft, sheer fabric often of silk or rayon yarns.

Chintz A cotton fabric, with or without a floral motif, with a glaze created by calendering and sometimes by adding a resin before calendering.

Ciré A high-luster glaze on silk, cotton, or synthetics, produced with wax or resins and hot rollers.

Colorfastness A general term denoting the relative durability of dye or pigment coloration to exposure to light, pollutants, or crocking and to laundering and cleaning processes.

Combing The process of laying long fibers parallel after carding and before spinning to produce a stronger, more lustrous yarn.

Compound cloth Cloths layered in two or more thicknesses, such as matelasse or Scotch ingrain.

Cord fabric A general term that refers to a fabric with a pronounced horizontal or vertical rib.

Cords and Ropes Cords are plied yarns that are twisted together, and when the diameter

Core A base yarn that is wrapped with a second and sometimes a third yarn element. The interior core is not visible in the finished cloth or passementerie.

Cotton A natural cellulosic seed-hair fiber obtained from the seedpod of the cotton plant. First known in India about 3000 B.C.

Crash A low-end cloth of slubby single-ply linen, cotton or synthetic yarn. Weavers use this also as a term for crushed polyester sheers.

Crêpe A general classification of fabrics that are characterized by a broad range of crinkled or grained surface effects. Methods of making crepe include the use of hard twisted yarns, special chemical treatment, special weaves and embossing.

Crewel A hand-embroidery technique from Kashmir in which fine, loosely twisted two-ply yarn is chain stitched on cotton cloth. Imperfections, color variations, irregularities, natural black specks, dye marks, and dirt spots are characteristics that label it as genuine. These fabrics are hand woven and embroidered by natives in India, and the beauty of the cloth is in its natural, homespun appearance.

Crimping A process in which natural or synthetic fibers are set in wavy coils for resilience, wrinkle resistance and natural cohesion in finishing.

Crocking The rubbing off of excess dyestuff from dry or wet fabric.

Cross dyeing Piece dyeing fabric that incorporates two generically different fibers with two different dyestuffs to produce checks, stripes or other combinations characteristic of yarn-dyed goods.

Crushed fabrics Pile fabrics, such as crushed velvet, crushed velour and plush, which are treated with heat, moisture and pressure in finishing to distort pile formation.

Cut order A fabric ordered to a specific measurement, as opposed to purchasing by the piece (a whole bolt).

"Neptune's Treasures" is printed on silk by Julio Zambrano using a semi-automatic flat bed carriage.

Color flags A series of swatches attached to a sample to show the complete colorline.

Colorline The range of available colors of a solid, printed or woven fabric.

Colorway An individual coloration from the full colorline.

Color value The lightness or darkness of a color.

exceeds one inch it is called a rope. Cords are used on furniture and cushions, usually with a cotton tape sewn onto the edge of the cord so it can be inserted in the upholstery seams. Cords are great to hot glue onto the edges of wall upholstery.

Corduroy A cut-pile fabric, usually cotton, in which the ribbed pile is produced with a supplementary weft yarn.

Cut pile   A fabric or carpet in which the pile is cut rather than looped, creating a velvet/velour effect.

Damask   Originally a rich silk fabric with woven floral designs made in China and introduced into Europe through Damascus, from which it derived its name. Typically, damasks are woven with a single beam (warp) and one or two weft colors. The fancy damasks of the seventeenth, eighteenth, nineteenth and twentieth centuries reveal the smooth-warp satin in the background with the low-luster reverse satin or twill in the motif. In two-color damasks, the colors reverse on either side. Single damask is made with a five-harness satin weave; the true, or double or reverse damask is woven with an eight-harness satin weave and has a firm hand.

Decatizing   A basic finishing process that amounts to a special type of light scouring and single calendering that improves the hand and luster of the cloth and sets the width. It may be used for wool, worsted and some other fibers. Also know as decating.

Degumming   The process of boiling off the natural gums from silk yarn or fabric.

Delustering   A chemical process in which the luster of man-made yarn or fabric is reduced by changing the character of its light reflection, either before spinning, by inserting colorless pigments into the solution, or during spinning, by altering the contour, cross section or density of a filament.

Denier   A unit of weight that indicates the size of a filament: the higher the denier, the heavier the yarn.

Denim   Yarn-dyed cotton cloth woven in a warp-faced twill, usually with a dyed warp and a natural weft.

Density   A standard measurement of thickness in fabric weight. Yarn size, amount of warp ends and weft picks determine the density.

Dent   The space between the teeth in the reed on a loom, which controls the spacing of the warp ends.

Developed dye   A dye that oxidizes and changes color after application.

Diaper   An allover repeating pattern produced by combining herringbone weave and a reversed twill.

Dimity   Fine cotton fabric made from alternating single, double or triple warp yarns that create small vertical stripes and often seersucker effects.

Direct dye   A class of dyes that are used for cellulosics and need no fixatives but have poor fastness.

Direct printing   A general term for a printing process in which color is applied directly onto the fabric.

Discharge printing   Method of printing with chlorine or other color-destroying chemicals on a fabric already dyed, so as to bleach out or discharge the color on the parts printed. This yields a white pattern on a colored ground. Colored patterns on a dyed ground are possible in this method by adding to the bleaching paste a dye not affected by the bleaching agent used, so that another color is created instead of white on the dyed ground. Synonym: Extract printing. *See* Resist Printing.

Dobby   A plain fabric woven on a dobby loom. A mechanical part of some plain looms that controls the harnesses to permit the weaving of small, geometric figures, i.e., dobby loom.

Dotted Swiss   A sheer cloth with a spaced pattern, produced by dense areas of supplementary weft in a swivel weave that creates raised dots.

Double cloth   A compound cloth based on two sets each of warp and weft held together at regular intervals by a warp or weft thread passing from one fabric to the other. Scotch ingrain is a great example.

Double-faced fabrics   A reversible fabric, usually with one set of warp yarns and two sets of weft yarns, one on each face.

Doupione   An irregular, slub silk reeled from double cocoons of silk caterpillars that have spun their cocoons side by side, causing an interlock, making it necessary to reel them together. Antique taffetas and sheers are woven with doupione weft yarn, as are many damasks. Also spelled *doupioni*.

Drill   A strong cloth, originally cotton, of twill construction.

Drugget   A fitted cloth often used under a dining table, on the bare floor or over another floor covering to catch the crumbs.

Duck   A broad term for a wide range of plain weave fabrics, duck is usually made of cotton, although sometimes linen is used. The terms *canvas* and *duck* are often used interchangeably, but *canvas* often is used to refer to the heavier constructions. The term *duck* had its origins before the mid-nineteenth century when all canvas for sails was imported. The light flax sail fabrics imported mostly from England and Scotland bore the trademark stencil of a raven, while the weights bore the trademark picturing a duck. *Duck* became associated with a heavy fabric and was applied to cotton canvas when it was first manufactured in the United States.

Emberling   A warp stripe often done in an exaggerated ombré effect. An emberling damask would have the striped warp as a background for the damask.

Embossing   A calendering process that produces a raised design or pattern in relief. The design is pressed into fabric by passing it through hot engraved rollers; velvet or plush is embossed by shearing the pile to different levels or by pressing parts flat. Special procedures recently developed produce a design or pattern that will not be removed by dampness, steam, washing, water spotting or dry cleaning.

End   A warp yarn.

End-and-end cloth   A plain-woven cloth, originally cotton, in which a textural pattern is produced by alternating ends of dark and light yarns. End-and-end warps are also used to enhance jacquard fabrics.

Epinglé   A French term meaning "pin," referring to a fine, lustrous, corded dress fabric with ribs running either warp-wise or weft-wise; the small ribs often alternate with heavier ribs. These raised, corded areas are created by weaving loop textures where yarns are woven over inserted wires, which are removed after weaving.

Fad-ometer   A machine that uses a carbon-arc ultraviolet light to test the relative resistance of fabrics or yarns to color loss in sunlight.

Faille   A lightweight fabric, originally silk, with a subtle horizontal rib. Belongs to the grosgrain class of textiles.

Fancy twill   A twill that requires eight or more harnesses to weave.

Fault   An eccentric characteristic or defect in a piece of cloth that may have a variety of causes.

Felt   A fabric made from fibers not taken to yarn form but instead intermeshed by heat, moisture and agitation. Felt is also a fabric made by shrinking and agitating woven or knit cloth to obtain superior density, resilience, strength, and a soft hand.

Fiberglass   A man-made mineral fiber extruded in continuous filaments.

Filament   A continuous strand of silk or man-made fiber.

Filling (Weft)   An element carried horizontally through the open shed of the vertical warp in a woven fabric.

Filouche   A French term for lightweight, sheer, plain-weave cotton fabric.

Finishes, functional or special   Treatments that are applied to fabrics to make them better suited for specific uses. These finishes include: Absorbent, Antibacterial, Crease Resistant, Durable Crease, Durable Press, Flame Resistant, Metalizing, Mildew Resistant, Moth Repellent, Shrinkage Control, Wash-and-Wear, Water Repellent, Waterproofing, etc.

Flame resistant fabric   A fabric whose fiber content or topical finish makes it difficult to ignite and slow to burn.

Flame-retardant fabric   A man-made fabric whose fiber content is officially acceptable for most fire code requirements, the idea being that in the event of fire, the flame-retardant fabric will not contribute to the flame.

Flannel   A woolen fabric whose surface is slightly napped in finish.

Flax   The plant from which linen is produced. The stem of the plant contains the bast fiber, which is extracted in the retting process to produce linen. An erroneous term for linen fiber, particularly in blends.

Float   The portion of a warp or weft yarn that rides over two or more opposing yarns to form a sleek face, as in satin, or is grouped to form a pattern on the face, as in brocade.

Flock   A very short wool, cotton, rayon or silk fiber created by grinding or cutting yarns, rags and clippings into a powder form that is used in flock printing.

Flock printing   Applying an adhesive to a fabric or paper surface, then applying flock to create a suede or velvet appearance. Sometimes the flock is electrically charges to create alignment of the fibers.

Floss   A strand made up of multiple plies of yarn filaments with only a slight twist to give maximum coverage and luster.

Fly   The contamination of a yarn or fabric by a foreign bit of color or fiber during spinning or weaving.

Fly-shuttle loom   A handloom in which the shuttle is shot through the warp shed by pulling a cord. Invented in 1738 by John Kay.

Foam   A man-made no-element fabric primarily used as a substrate or backing for another fabric.

Frame   Technical grading of certain types of carpets, such as Brussels and Wilton. The number of frames used indicates the amount of pile yarn imbedded in the fabric. The frames are placed at the back of the loom and are arranged one on top of the other; they are racks of creel-like trays that hold the spools of pile yarn. Up to six frames may be used. The spools in any one frame generally contain the same color of yarn, although planting is sometimes done. Generally speaking, five-frame Wilton carpets contain five colors.

Friezé   A warp-pile fabric with uncut loops for upholstery. Commonly the pile is mohair or wool worsted.

Fringe   Fringe is a narrow-width woven or knitted decorative fabric with a heading and attached skirt. The height or length of fringe varies from one to eighteen inches.

Frogs   Frogs are wrapped cord or silk-covered wire made into a series of loops; these are often combined with tassels and are used like rosettes.

Fulling   A finishing operation dependent on the felting property of wool, that shrinks the fabric to make it heavier and thicker.

Fusing   A process in which thermoplastic fibers or yarns are melted together, as in ribbons, or heat-sealed, as in joinings, to form a fused edge.

Fustian   Originates in the Fustat, old Arab quarters of Cairo. Cotton and linen were used.

Gabardine   A worsted cloth characterized by a sharp, diagonal twill and a polished surface.

Gassing   Process of burning off protruding fibers from cotton yarns.

Gauffrage   The French term for the process of embossing.

Gauze   An openly constructed, transparent cloth of any fiber.

Gimp   A silk or metallic yarn spiral wrapped closely around an inner core to cover it completely to create a slightly rigid cord. Also, a narrow braid used to cover tacks or staples in upholstery.

Gingham   A yarn-dyed, combed or carded cotton fabric woven into a series of simple patterns—such as checks, stripes or plaids—in two or more colors.

Glass curtains   Very sheer curtains hanging over windows, usually under draperies.

Glazing   A general term for a polished finish on a cloth, often using waxes or resins and hot rollers.

Gobelin   The Gobelin family, famous for dyeing, settled in Paris in the fifteenth century. When a factory for tapestry weaving was established in 1662 in Paris, it consolidated individual studios and assumed the name "Gobelin." Genuine Gobelin is made with bobbins and the different colored yarns extend only as far as required by the design, rather than from selvage to selvage. This term is also used for loom-woven fabrics that simulate hand gobelins.

Grass cloth   A broad classification for lustrous, plain-weave fabrics made of ramie, flax, hemp, nettle fiber grass, etc. It generally is loosely woven on hand looms in the Orient and adhered to paper grounds.

Grain   The alignment of vertical and horizontal elements in a fabric, approaching a right-angle relationship. It is recommended to upholster fabrics with the grain (such as satin weaves or repps).

Gray goods (Greige) Knitted or woven fabrics of all fibers in an unfinished state (before conversion); after they have been woven (loom state) and before dyeing or finishing. Referred to as "greige goods" or "in the greige", it was derived from the French word *beige* for 'natural.' While greige is used to some degree for silk and man-made fabrics, there is a tendency toward the use of the word *gray* instead.

Grin A small area of ground color that shows through. This may occur if the print is off-register, or if a velvet ground varies in color from the nap or when yarns spread apart.

Grosgrain A firm, closely woven ribbed fabric in full width or ribbon. It is woven in a plain or variation of the plain weave. A large number of warp ends per inch are employed to cover the heavier weft yarns completely.

Grospoint A heavy cloth woven to resemble the large needle stitch (grospoint) in hand embroidery.

Halftone Subtle shading from one color to another; usually a value change from dark to light of the same color.

Halo A partially dyed area around the pattern of a discharge print, or a reflection of the pattern that occurs in the moiré of a woven design.

Part of the Jacquard includes chains that align and time the motion of the punch cards through the machine.

Hand Literally, the feel of the goods in the hand; a qualitative term used to describe the tactile properties of a fabric.

Hand printing A variety of pre-industrial printing techniques that are done by hand, including resist, block, and screen prints.

Hank See skein.

Harlequin A large check turned 45 degrees to form a diamond in two or more contrasting colors; suggested by the loudly checked costume of a harlequin.

Harness The part of the loom containing the heddles through which warp yarns are threaded.

Heat transfer printing A method that transfers designs from rolls of paper to polyester or other thermo-plastic fibers. Designs are preprinted with disperse dyes on paper, and under high temperature of 400 degrees F, are transferred onto fabric when both are passed through a heat transfer printing machine. Disperse dyes are the only ones that can sublimate and therefore are the only ones that can be used. An adaptation of the decalcomania method.

Hemp A high-strength bast fiber.

Herringbone A twill weave that reverses direction across the fabric to form a chevron.

Homespun A clubby, single-ply yarn with some of the random character of hand spun yarn.

Honan A lustrous tussah silk, originally hand woven in the Honan province of China.

Honeycomb A piqué weave in a hexagonal shape. Often referred to as a waffle weave.

Hopsacking A coarse, loose, plain- or basket-woven fabric of cotton or other yarns.

Horsehair A long, lustrous hair obtained from the mane and tail of a horse. Length varies from 8 inches to 3 feet; colors range from natural tan to brown and black. Longer hairs are used as the weft yarn in narrow-width fabrics (between 24 and 26 inches), the shortest hair for brushes and also curled for stuffing furniture and mattresses. During the nineteenth century, horsehair fabric was very popular and widely used for upholstery in plain,

both, and called warp ikat, weft ikat or double ikat, respectively. A technique of great antiquity, which developed in northeastern Asia. The characteristic designs are created by carefully distorting the resists before weaving.

Indian cotton A general term for varieties of cotton grown in India and Pakistan. For centuries India was the leading cotton producer of the world, but now it ranks fourth, superseded by the United States, Russia and China in the quantity grown. Although cotton has been grown there for thousands of years, no effort

Indian cotton include the short staples Bengal and Ooma cottons; and the medium and long staple Punjab, Cambodia and Broach. Indian cotton is often designated by the name of the region where it is grown.

Indian import Due to the fact that these fabrics are hand woven in a method unchanged for centuries, the yardage varies from lot to lot. There can be no standardization. The yarns themselves vary greatly. There is no formula dye, rather it is dyed by sight only. Streaking is always possible due to different penetration of color. The looms have foot pedals that pull up the shafts, and the shuttle is drawn through by hand. The tension of the weft yarn depends solely on how tightly the yarn is pulled by the weaver. Request clippings before proceeding with order.

Cheerful yellow and red cones of acrylic yarn hang on a creel while a warper transfers the yarn from the cones to the warping wheel.

Ingrain A term that indicates a yarn was dyed before being woven or knitted. This also refers to an intricate loomed carpet referred to as Scotch Ingrain.

Interlining A layer of fabric between the outer decorative fabric and the lining.

Iridescent A color effect created by weaving warp ends of one color and a weft of another color. The taffeta weave creates the best iridescent effects.

Jacquard A system of weaving that because of a pattern-making mechanism of great versatility, permits the production of woven designs of considerable size. The Jacquard

dobby and jacquard designs. Horsehair is also referred to as haircloth.

Hound's-tooth check A pointed check effect produced by a two up, two down broken twill with four ends and four picks in a repeat.

Ikat A resist form of fabric decoration. A textile fabric is called an ikat when the yarn is tie-dyed for dyeing and weaving purposes, as distinct from tie-dyeing the whole fabric. Derived from the Malayan word *mengilat,* meaning to tie, knot, bind or wind around. The ikat technique can be applied to the warp, the weft or

was made to improve the Indian varieties until around the time of the American Civil War, when the industry was stimulated by the temporary loss of the American cotton on the world market. The Deccan region of central India is the largest producing cotton area. Cotton for export is primarily shipped from Bombay. The finest variety of the Indian cottons was the Dacca cotton grown in Bengal, which is today part of Pakistan. The Dacca area of Pakistan still grows a fine variety of cotton but produces no yarn or woven fabric as fine as the original hand-spun, hand-woven Dacca cottons. The better-known varieties of

loom, a derivation of the old draw-boy handloom, was credited to Joseph Marie Jacquard in France in the early nineteenth century. There were others who attempted to perfect the process during the late eighteenth century; however, J. M. Jacquard finally patented the design of the head motion of the loom. In this system of weaving, the weave pattern is copied from the design paper by punching a series of cards, each perforation controlling the action of one warp thread for the passage of one pick. The machine may carry a large number of cards, depending upon the design, because there is a separate card for each pick. Today, Jacquard looms can be controlled electronically by computer, allowing for unlimited vertical repeats. The average dobby loom, which activates a series of threads by means of harnesses, is limited in weave effects to a pattern in which the total different effects are about thirty at the most. On the Jacquard loom, because the threads are handled individually, anywhere from 100 to 15,000 threads may have independent weave action, allowing for complicated curvilinear designs. This system of weaving is used for brocade, brocatelle, damask, lampas, liseré, matelassé, tapestry and many other types of figured materials.

Jaspé   Each country, and often each mill, uses this term differently. For over sixty-five years, Scalamandré has used the following description: "A shaded effect in the fabric created by irregularly mixing warp yarns which are different shades of a color, or different colors."

Jig dyeing   A form of piece dyeing in which an open width of cloth is repeatedly run through a stationary dye bath.

Jobber   A mercantile company that buys large lots of fabric from a producer or converter and wholesales in smaller quantities.

Jute   A bast fiber obtained from the round-pod jute *(corchorus capsularis)* or the long-pod jute *(corchorus olitorius)* of the family *Tiliaceae.* Grown extensively in Pakistan and India, mainly in the Bengal district of Pakistan.

Kilim   A pileless tapestry-woven carpet, mat or spread.

Knitting   A method of constructing fabric by interlocking series of loops of one or more yarns. Three classes of knit fabrics are circular knit, flat knit and warp knit.

Knot   Any area where yarns are joined.

Lace   An open-work fabric produced by a network of threads twisted together, and sometimes knotted, to form patterns. It is made by hand with bobbins and pins (bobbinet or pillow lace), with needles (needlepoint or point lace), with hooks (tatting), or by machinery.

Lambrequin   A rigid or soft covering over the upper portion of a window or door.

Lamé   Any fabric woven with flat metallic threads or tinsel that form either the ground or the pattern. Derived from the French word *lamé,* which means "trimmed with leaves of gold or silver."

Laminated fabric   Fabric created by bonding two or more layers of material together.

Lampas   Jacquard fabric made with two or more warps and two or more wefts. A dramatic and saturated two-tone effect can be obtained when each color warp weaves with the same color weft. As many as 18,000 ends may be across the warp. The weft is used to create the pattern and achieve a multicolored pattern effect and was popularized in France during the eighteenth century. The original lampases were woven of silk, but a variety of yarns are used today.

Lampas with brocade effect   Woven on a lampas loom, this fabric weaves so that the weft yarn floats on top in a twill effect and floats in the back across the width of the fabric. A taffeta ground is possible in this weave, whereas a satin, or twill, effect is woven in the background in a lampas weave.

Lawn   Sheer, crisp cotton or linen in plain weave between voile and organdy.

Leno weave   A weaving process in which two or more warp yarns are twisted by a mechanism added to the loom. The weft is shot straight across the fabric as in a plain weave, but the warp threads are alternately twisted in a right- and left-hand direction, crossing before each pick is inserted. This weave gives firmness and strength to an open-weave cloth, preventing slipping and displacements of warp and weft yarns. Synonym: doup weave.

Linen   Strong, lustrous yarn made from flax fiber.

Linsey   Cloth made of linen and woolen yarn. Cotton is sometimes used with or in place of linen.

Liseré   Jacquard fabric in which the warp threads of a second beam are usually used to float on top of the cloth to create the design. Liseré's may be multicolored, or one color may be placed on the second beam.

Loom state   Goods as they come off the loom before converting or finishing.

Macramé   Hand needlework employing a variety of knots that create an open-weave fancy netting.

Madras   Plain cotton cloth, usually in strong-colored plaids or checks, that originated in Madras, India. Also refers to a jacquard cloth woven in Scotland with a twisted gauze weave created by using two reeds, one working against the other. The floating weft is cut away, leaving a pattern outline on a sheer cloth.

Marcella   Also called Marseille Quilt, is an all-white, elaborately corded quilt usually made of silk or linen, although cotton and wool are also used. Originally made by hand in Marseille, France, the English began producing Marcellas on looms by the late eighteenth century.

Martindale test   An English test used by the Wool Bureau for testing abrasion resistance.

Marquisette   A leno-woven sheer often used for glass curtains.

Matelassé   The French word *Matelasser* means "to quilt, to pad." This fabric is woven with two warps, which in weaving, achieves a puckered or quilted effect.

Melton   A heavy, felted, dark-colored cloth, often of reprocessed wool.

Mercerizing   A process that gives luster and strength to yarn or cloth.

Metamerism   A term that refers to matching or mismatching of color samples under various light sources. A metameric match is when two different lot samples of the same design/color look good in one light and don't match under a second illuminant.

Meter   A universally accepted measurement based in hundreds. It is equivalent to 39.37 inches. This measurement is used in the majority of the world, although the yard is still used in the USA and England.

Mohair   A long, white, lustrous hair obtained from the Angora goat. A mohair plush is a fabric with a cut pile of mohair yarns. It is lustrous and extremely strong and will hold a permanent embossing.

Moiré   A French word meaning "watered." A three-part finishing process that produces a wavy or rippling pattern on the fabric. Each fabric moirés differently, and a test run of a minimum of twenty yards must be done to estimate the production result. Both natural and man-made fibers can be used to create moiré fabrics.

Monk's cloth   Made of coarse cotton or linen yarns, generally a basket weave.

Moreen   A moiréd fabric of wool or wool blends.

Muslin   A plain-weave strong cotton cloth.

Napping   A finishing process in which circular brushes vigorously raise the fiber ends, forming a pilelike surface.

Natural fibers   A general term for fibers derived from natural substances such as cellulose, proteins and minerals.

Net   A general term for a lacy, diamond-shaped mesh.

Noil   A short fiber or waste silk made from leftovers of the silk processing called sericulture. It has a dull surface and informal appearance. *See* Bourette.

Nylon   A generic term for the synthetic polyamide fibers.

Olefin   A man-made fiber composed of at least 85 percent by weight of ethylene, propylene or other olefin units.

Ombré   A shaded, striped effect is created in the warp by graduating the shades of the warp yarns from light to dark. Usually a group of warp threads are dyed one color, then a smaller group dyed a lighter shade of the same color, etc.

Organdy   A sheer cotton fabric made of fine count, combed singles in open, plain weave with characteristic stiff, crisp, clear finish.

Organza   A thin, transparent silk, rayon or nylon fabric made in a plain weave and given a stiff, wiry finish.

Organzine   Made by twisting together single filaments from eight to ten silk cocoons and given sixteen turns per inch. This yarn is usually plied (twisted) again with another and used for warp yarn.

Ottoman   A firm, lustrous, plain-weave fabric with horizontal cords that are larger and rounder than those of faille or bengaline. Silk, cotton, wool or man-made fibers are used, and cotton is sometimes employed in the weft, which is completely covered by the warp. Jacquard ottoman combines complex figured motifs with an ottoman ground.

Oxford cloth   Plain, basket or twill weave in a cotton or rayon cloth.

Panama cloth   A plain-weave fabric often of a cotton warp and wool weft.

Panné   A French word meaning "shag, plush." A pile fabric with a long pile. The pile is flattened or pressed down by means of heavy roller pressure in finishing, giving the fabric a high luster.

Panné satin   A high-luster fabric created by a special finish.

Passementerie   French word meaning "trimming," as in braids, gimps, tassels and cords.

Percale   A fine, plain-woven cloth of closely set combed and carded long-staple cotton.

Pick   One weft of yarn or yarns, passed through the cloth when a shed is created by lifting specific warp yarns.

Pigment   An insoluble powdered coloring agent carried in a liquid binder and printed or padded onto the surface of a cloth.

Piece dyeing   A process of dyeing fabric in the piece (also known as bolt).

Pile   Raised loops, cut interlacings of double cloths or tufts (cut loops), and other erect yarns or fibers deliberately produced on cloth, that form all or part of the surface above the fabric ground.

Pill   A fuzzy ball caused by the rolling up of abraded surface fibers.

Pima cotton   Extra-long-staple fiber with a silky sheen. Originally named for Pima County, Arizona.

Piqué   Fabric has an embossed appearance created by weaving ribbed, waffle or honeycomb patterns.

Plain weave   One up, one down construction, sometimes referred to as a tabby or taffeta weave.

Plissé   A puckered or blistered design effect formed by shrinking fabric in selected areas with a caustic soda solution (cotton) or heat (synthetics).

Plush   A warp pile fabric with a thick, soft-cut pile surface longer than velvet pile and less closely woven using natural or synthetic fibers.

Ply   The number of yarns twisted together to make a composite yarn.

Pocket weave   A double cloth in which the two cloth layers are joined only at the pattern change.

Polyester   A generic term for a manufactured fiber in which the fiber-forming substance is a long-chain synthetic polymer composed of a complex ester.

Pongeé   A plain-woven cloth usually woven with tussah silk of various natural colors.

Poplin   A plain-woven, warp-faced fabric with a fine crosswise rib running from selvage to selvage.

Protein fibers   A general term for natural fibers derived from animal protein, such as wool, silk, and hair; animal protein is also used for various man-made fibers produced from casein bases.

Quadrille   A French term for small checked patterns, such as shepherd's checks.

Raffia   A leaf stalk fiber obtained from the raffia palm in Raffia, Madagascar.

Railroad   To upholster a cloth by turning it 90 degrees so the vertical warp yarns run horizontally.

Ramie   Ramie is a grass similar to flax fiber. It is very strong, lustrous and white.

Raw silk   Silk fiber or fabric that has not had the sericin (or gum) boiled off.

Rayon   Generic term for a man-made fiber derived from regenerated cellulose.

Reactive dyes   A class of dyes that react chemically with fiber molecules and produce fast, bright colors.

Reed The comblike device on a loom through which all warp yarns are entered.

Reed mark A vertical streak in woven fabric caused by a bent wire in the reed. Stripes are sometimes designed into a cloth by special reed entries.

Reeled silk Continuous-filament silk as it is reeled off the softened cocoon of the cultivated silkworm.

Repp (Rep) weave A fabric with closely spaced narrow ribs running horizontally in the direction of the weft. The ribs are more distinct than a faille and less dramatic than an ottoman.

Repeat An entire repeated pattern. Most figured patterns have a vertical and a horizontal repeat.

Repoussé A hammered or pressed pattern effect.

Resin A synthetic substance used in corrective finishes to add body, reduce creasing, control shrinkage, produce luster in glazing, repel water, or supply permanent press.

Resin finish Chemicals such as formaldehyde or melamine are applied to cloth, then heat set, to create a variety of finishes such as water-repellent, wrinkle resistant, glaze, etc.

Resist printing The design desired is printed on the fabric with a material that will resist dyeing. The fabric is then piece dyed. Washing removes the resisted colorant in the design area, leaving a white pattern. A different color may be applied in the resist paste. This is the reverse of discharge printing.

"Galapagos," a contemporary acrylic jacquard from the outdoor Island Cloth Collection is being woven on a mechanical Jacquard loom.

Rib weave A variation of the plain weave that produces ribs running in the direction of the warp or weft by having two or more successive ends or picks weave alike, i.e., ends alternating under and over two or more picks, or picks alternating under and over two or more ends. Ribs are also produced by employing coarser yarn for the rib than for the ground.

Roller printing A method of printing fabric with engraved wood or metal rollers.

Rosettes Rosettes are handmade from fabrics that have been concentrically gathered to resemble a rose, and are used on the corners of cushions, swags and tassels. Rosettes can also be fabric-covered cardboard cutouts shaped into flowers.

Lustrous blue silk threads are wound onto wooden spools for the warping department.

Rotary printing A method of printing with continuous circular screens. Colorants are pumped inside the cylinder and then forced through to the surface of the screen.

Rouche: (also ruche) A gathered strip of fabric used in trimming, usually along the vertical edges of the construction.

Satin This weave is usually made with five, eight or ten shafts that have the warp yarn float the same number of times above the weft, then bound once before floating again. The weave produces a fabric with a characteristic smooth surface, and high luster. Weft, or filler, satins are usually referred to as sateens.

Screen printing Somewhat like stencil printing, where a frame stretched with a fine mesh has all areas of the mesh covered, except where the color is to be pressed through. A squeegee is passed across the screen to push the color through to the cloth.

Seersucker A plain-woven cloth, often striped, with puckered or blistered vertical rows produced by a shrinking differential in two groups of warp yarns.

Selvage The edge on either side of a woven or flat-knitted fabric, often of different threads and/or weave, so finished to prevent raveling. Special selvages are often necessary for special finishing processes.

Serge A solid color twill that creates a fine diagonal pattern, often woven in worsted wool.

Shaf Another name for a harness on a loom through which warp yarns are passed.

Shantung A lightweight silk cloth woven in a plain weave with doupioni yarn (a slubby silk yarn).

Shed The triangular opening between the raised and lowered warp ends through which the weft yarns pass.

Sheer A very thin, transparent or semi-opaque fabric.

Sheeting Plain-woven cotton of various qualities, the traditional ground for chintz and a basic cloth for printing.

Shuttle A device that carries the weft yarn across the width of a loom.

Shuttleless loom A loom in which the weft is carried across by means other than a shuttle.

Silk A natural protein fiber produced from the cocoon of wild or cultivated silkworms.

Silk floss Short fibers of tangled waste silk.

Silksy-Woolsey A silk and woolen fabric.

Sisal or sisal hemp A strong, coarse leaf fiber used primarily for cord and carpeting.

Sizing A process of applying a finish to the warp prior to weaving in order to enhance production. It is removed in finishing.

Skein A loosely coiled length of yarn or thread wound on a reel. Also referred to as a "hank."

Slub yarn   A novelty yarn with soft, thick, untwisted lengths that alternate regularly with thin places in the thread. The slubs can be made during spinning, or appear in natural silk doupioni yarns.

Slippage   A fabric fault caused by warp and weft yarns sliding on each other. In most instances, the problem can be remedied by increasing the pick count.

Solution dyeing   Color is introduced into man-made fibers in a pre-extrusion state that achieves excellent colorfastness.

Space dyeing   Dyeing a yarn so that various parts of the same skein are different colors, or various shades of a color.

Spolinato   Means "hand brocade" in Italian. This term is derived from the word *spolino* which means "shuttle." The fabric is woven with one or more warps. The ground of the fabric is woven by warp and weft while the design is woven by weaving in and out of the warp threads by hand, with a hand shuttle. This fabric weaves a few inches a day.

Spun silk   Yarn twisted from silk waste or pierced cocoons. Degumming must occur prior to spinning.

Stock dyeing   A method of introducing color into stock prior to spinning the yarn that achieves excellent color uniformity.

Strie   A narrow streak or stripe effect that can run vertically, horizontally or both. Most Italian mills, including the Scalamandré factory, create warp stries by space dyeing the skeins in two or three shades of a particular hue (color). After weaving, the vertical effect is subtle; however, one should be able to see the darker streaks dark to light while following that particular yarn up the length of the fabric. Many of our French suppliers refer to a warp strie when two to three different-colored warp ends are planted irregularly across the width of the fabric. This is a technique some mills call jaspé.

Suede cloth   Sheeting napped on one side to resemble leather suede.

Sultane   Named for the first wife of a sultan. Made of a silk warp and wool weft with a twill weave, it is then given a rough finish.

Tabby weave   One up, one down weave. Same as plain or taffeta weaves. **Taffeta**   A French term used to describe a tightly woven, crisp, plain silk. Silk blends and synthetics can also be made into taffeta. This is the simplest weave—one thread up, one thread down—also called a plain or unbalanced tabby weave. Rich silk taffeta has scroop and sounds like a person walking on freshly fallen snow. Antique taffeta is a taffeta weave using doupioni yarn.

Tambour curtains   Panels of heavily embroidered sheer curtains.

Tapestry   In hand-woven tapestry, the image is created by numerous discontinuous wefts along each row. The weft threads are generally woven area by area and shape by shape, as opposed to other woven forms where the weft travels from edge to edge across the width of the warp as on a Jacquard loom. The motifs are created, manipulating up to five or six warp colors using wefts of white and black.

Tartan   Multicolored plaids originally made for Scottish clan kilts.

Tassels   Tassels are hanging trims that have a head and skirt of cut yarn or bullion cord. Tassels are often combined with other trim such as cord, rosettes, frogs and heading. They can be used on pillow corners, furniture, bell pulls and on drapery swags between looped cords.

Throwing   The actual twisting, without drawing, of continuous fibers or filaments.

Ticking   A general term for a strong, durable, closely woven striped fabric in plain, twill or satin weave, which is used for covering box springs, mattresses and pillows.

Tieback   Can be made with fabric, with open-scroll braid, or with cords that are either single or double stranded and often have tassels at the ends. Tiebacks are used to hold back drapery treatments.

Tie-dyeing   Areas of the cloth or yarn are tightly tied into a knot so that when the cloth or yarn is dyed, parts of the cloth will not receive the dye and an irregular pattern is created.

Tissue   A lightweight cloth. Also a weft term for motif yarn that is used to put a point of color to the face of the fabric and are loose on the back. The weft is intermittent on the back,

not continuous as in a brocade.

Tobacco cloth   A lightweight, unsized, loosely plain woven cotton fabric used to cover tobacco plants, a similar cloth is used to wrap food and is known as cheesecloth.

Toile   A French word for cloth or fabric, linen, sailcloth, canvas. The linen or cotton cloth was made famous when a new technique of engraved plate printing was popularized in Jouy, France, in the eighteenth century. The finished printed cloth was referred to as toile de Jouy. Today it usually describes a one-color, fine-line printed design that resembles a pen-and-ink technique. Toiles are printed by various methods, but the most beautiful are still created by engraved plates or rollers. Historical and classical motifs are the norm.

Top dyeing   A form of stock dyeing in which a loose rope of parallel wool fibers is dyed prior to spinning. Also known as stock dyeing. Top dyeing also refers to a dye house dyeing or tinting an already dyed bolt of fabric.

Tram   Silk yarn with very few turns per inch. It is a lustrous yarn used as a weft.

Transfer printing   A technique whereby the fabric is printed in color on large rolls of paper. This printed design on paper is pressed against the fabric and transferred to it. Application of heat and pressure transfers the design to the fabric and the color is set. Often called dry transfer printing. A new technique is wet transfer printing. This involves padding the substrate with a carrier to increase its affinity for the dyes on the paper. *See also* Heat transfer printing.

Tricot   A plain-warp knitted fabric with a close, inelastic vertical knit.

Tufting   A wide, multiple-machine needle process that sews pile yarns to a broad fabric backing of cotton, canvas or jute. A popular method of constructing tufted rugs. A piece of yarn is pushed through the fabric, caught by a latch and held, and then withdrawn through the fabric. The tuft may be either loop or cut pile, and sometimes combinations of both loop and cut are employed for a design effect. Tufting is a decorative technique in upholstering whereby recessed buttons, bows or rosettes are applied.

Tufts   Tufts are circular groupings of yarn that have been looped and banded at the center, and the ends are sometimes cut. Tufts can be used on upholstery and other ornamentation.

Tulle A sheer cloth woven with a hexagonal mesh; it is stiff and often used for ballet costumes.

Tunnel test Known as the E-84 Tunnel Test; often specified for testing the flame retardancy of wallcoverings.

Tussah A brownish silk yarn or fabric made from wild silk cocoons of a brownish color. These caterpillars primarily feed on leaves from oak plants and trees.

Tweed A homespun effect created by multi- or monochromatic colored yarns woven on plain looms. The fabric is usually wool or worsted and often has a rough texture.

Twill This is a weave that creates a diagonal effect by having the warp float on top of a few weft yarns, or vice versa. Generally three threads up and one down. Antique twill is woven as a twill with a doupioni yarn, having slubs intermittently dispersed across the fabric.

Twisting Winding two or more strands of fiber or yarn together to make a single multiple-ply thread or yarn. Also the term used in weaving for knotting a new warp onto a loom.

Vat dyeing A dyeing process in which alkaline-soluble dyes are oxidized to produce excellent colorfastness in cellulosic fibers.

Vegetable fibers All-natural fibers from plants such as cotton, flax, ramie, jute, hemp, abaca, sisal, etc.

Velour A fabric with a pile or napped surface resembling velvet. Now loosely applied to cut pile fabrics in general.

Velvet There are two basic types of velvets: plain and figured. The pile in any velvet always comes from a supplemental warp beam raised above the ground weave and manipulated over rods during the weaving process. (continued)When the rods are removed, the looped pile or piles may be cut or uncut.

1. The hand-woven velvet is produced by inserting a rod with a groove cut into it under the warp on each pick of the loom. The warp threads form loops, which are then cut by hand. Variation of length of pile is caused by any slight movement up or down by the human hand that cuts the pile.

2. Single-layer machine-woven velvet.

3. The automatically woven velvet can be a double-faced fabric. It weaves two fabrics, face to face, joined by the weft yarns. These yarns are then cut automatically, which forms the pile on both faces.

Velveteen A fabric with a single weft, similar to velvet but generally much softer and used for apparel. The pile is created by the weft yarn.

Venitienne A silk fabric originally made in Venice and copied in France in the seventeenth century. Made plain or figured with gold and silver, generally in large, trailing designs. During the early nineteenth century, figured repps called Venitienne were made in cotton and wool, then by the middle of the century silk was used in Venitienne.

Vermicelli A printed, woven, embroidered or quilted technique that produces an overall pattern of noodlelike squiggles. Often referred to as a pattern with squiggly lines.

Vicuña A small, wild Andean llama from the undercoat of which a fine, lustrous fiber is derived.

Virgin wool New wool of any grade.

Voided velvet A single woven velvet with an intaglio pattern incised in the ground cloth.

Voile A soft, sheer cloth plain woven of fine crepe-spun yarns.

W-construction In a pile weave, catching the pile yarns under one weft and over another and tying them down on the third to keep them from pulling out of the face of the cloth. More durable than the "V" weave for velvets.

Warp Yarns placed on a warp beam and entered into a loom. The yarns stretched through the length of a loom will become the foundation of the fabric.

Warp print Warp threads are arranged in the same order as they will lie in the finished cloth and are printed before weaving. The process involves many intricate steps that include preparing the yarns and making a warp, weaving with very few weft yarns, then printing the warp. Setting the color, reentering, cutting out the first wefts and finally reweaving the cloth.

Waste silk Short, unreeled filaments that remain before and after the long filaments are reeled. These are spun into silk noil, bourette and spun silk.

Weaving The art of interlacing both warp and weft yards at right angles to produce a woven fabric.

Weft Often referred to as "filling," it is the yarn that traverses the warp yarns (horizontally) during the weaving operation.

Weighted silk Metallic salts are added to silk yarn to return the weight artificially, after the boiling-off process of the sericin. Artificial weighting is prohibited in the United States as it results in poor-quality yarn. Unfortunately, there are global areas that still use weighting.

Wilton carpet A cut-pile carpet woven on a Jacquard loom, made with wool or worsted, or wool nylon blends. Made with three to six frames. Worsted Wilton is considered the best carpet made, and can be distinguished from wool Wilton by the short pile and tightly woven back. This quality originated in Wilton, England, and continues to be woven twenty-seven inches wide. There are wider widths as well.

Woof Same as weft.

Wool Fibers that grow on the sheep known as fleece. There are varieties of wool such as Alpaca, Angora, Botany, Cashmere, Merino and Shetland.

Worsted Choice woolen stock made from long fibers of approximately the same length.

Yard A 36-inch measure in America. The American yard is 1/100,000 of an inch longer than the English yard.

FACING *A blotch screen for "Jackson Floral" with buckets of dyestuff, is ready for production and shows the intricacy involved in hand printing.*

Continuous yellow plastic punch cards are used in some of the modern mechanical Jacquard looms.